THE BADGE

THE BADGE

ASHLEY TOPHAM

First published in 2014 on behalf of the author by

Scotforth Books (www.scotforthbooks.com)

ISBN   978-1-909817-07-4

Typesetting and design by Carnegie Book Production, Lancaster.

Printed in the UK by Short Run Press

I am fit and well trained;
I work hours that would break most men.

My hands can be the most gentle you have held,
or strong when I carry a comrade from danger.

I fight in faraway places for those
who cannot fight for themselves.

When asked if I was a hero I reply no,
but served with a regiment of heroes.

*This book is dedicated to my brother Paul Topham, who died
in Malaya. For his life I experienced mine.*

Contents

CHAPTER ONE

Training

Many books have been written by high-ranking officers and men from the Special Forces. There are books about every military conflict where the British Army has been involved, full of tales of how individuals single-handedly took on hundreds of the enemy. If you go in to any bookshop the shelves are filled with these magnificent stories of courageous men and their great experiences, some traumatic and some uplifting.

This book is about me, a normal soldier in a normal regiment. I served for twenty three years and ten months, reaching the rank of Warrant Officer Class One, Regimental Sergeant Major (RSM). The contents of my book describe the experience of war, including the humiliation and turmoil of my capture, which caused an international incident and reached the in-tray of the Prime Minister.

My memories are of comradeship, humour and loyalty, and on the reverse, bullying and fighting. This happens between men in the Army all over the world and points out the courage and commitment it takes to serve despite what is pitted against you. I have been inspired to write my own account of my experience because of the incredible luck, bad and good, that anyone can encounter in a lifetime. My story magnifies and shows how we never know what's around the corner, be it an intense low or an incredible natural high.

I hope this story is as enjoyable for you to read as it has been for me to write it. It will make you laugh. For those who have not served it will give you an insight in to a soldier's life; for those who have, it will give you memories of the experience you had.

On leaving the forces each soldier is given a red folder which contains the history of his service and a final report for him to take away to help with his future. This gives a description of his final rank; it's to help him in Civilian Street when we go for a job interview. It allows the new employer to understand a little about the man standing in front of him. This is the extract that describes a Warrant Officer Class One, Regimental Sergeant Major:

> He is responsible for the implementation
> of the Commanding Officer's policy on
> discipline. Supervises the Commanding
> Officer's summary jurisdiction parades,
> advises Warrant Officers and Senior NCOs
> on matters of discipline and military law,
> and directs the custody of prisoner and those
> under sentence. Responsible for the conduct
> of the unit personnel, including attached
> civilian staffs. Responsible for unit parades.
> As an administrator co-ordinates the day-
> to-day administrative duties within the unit
> or barracks, which include such matters as
> cleanliness and security. Carries out inspec-
> tions with or on behalf of the Commanding
> Officer. Takes a particular interest in
> all sporting, social and welfare matters,
> frequently advising or acting on behalf of the

Commanding Officer. Normally advises the Commanding Officer on the promotion of NCOs. Assists in the training of Junior NCOs. On training or operations will carry out additional duties as prescribed by the unit, which normally include the sitting defence and security of the headquarters and acting as or duty liaison officer. Will be expected to take command and interpret battle plans in the absence of an officer. As the senior Warrant Officer of the unit has a special responsibility for the conduct and administration of the Warrant Officers' and Sergeants' Mess, including supervising the financial account. May also direct the administration of the Junior NCO Mess. ONLY A FEW SENIOR WARRANT OFFICERS are selected for this appointment through long experience and above average previous performance. Holds a position of considerable responsibility and used to dealing with all ranks in a variety of circumstances.

To sum up, it means he is the top soldier and has done extremely well to make it to this rank and appointment, in my opinion a shit hot specimen of a guy! He has been chosen from a cast of highly motivated competition. Soldiers would say, 'watch out, the Badge is coming!' Officers would say the only man that scared them was the RSM. It is not the man, but the badge: the power of wearing the rank produces the respect. Most men who have had the privilege to wear the badge are the nicest people you could meet, however when that badge is on their arm, they can also be the most scary bastard ever.

I left the Army as Regimental Sergeant Major. I achieved this rank by hard work and of course luck and being in the right place at the right time. In my opinion lots of soldiers deserve to reach this rank but sometimes don't, partly I believe due to bad luck and possibly being in the wrong place at the wrong time. In my experience I think it was commonly due to an individual not liking them and giving them a report that knocked them back on the promotion board. I can honestly say that I served with some great soldiers who were better than I was but who did not make the rank. I joined as a young lad, starting at the bottom of the ladder, and finished at the top as a Regimental Sergeant Major, the top soldier in a British Army Regiment. Out of every 15,000 men who join the Army, only one man makes it to RSM.

It all started one warm summer's morning in 1980. I lay in bed for about five minutes procrastinating about getting up and facing the day. Then like something I'd never felt before, I HAD AN URGE TO DO IT. I was going to Lincoln and was going to join the British Army. I was fifteen years old, weighed eight stone and was five foot six. I finally felt ready and I knew I had the guts to do it.

I was a good sportsman; I'd had rugby trials for the county and represented my school at football as well. I was bit of a Jack the lad and was constantly told by my peers that I would not make it in life. I messed about at school and never took it seriously. I really did not like school life and looked forward to the bell sounding for the end of the day and getting out of there. I remember one time when they told us the scores of one of our mock exams, my mate scored just one. I was laughing so much I fell off my chair, until the teacher said, 'I don't know what you are laughing at Topham, you have scored zero!'

I spent most of my time in trouble and was always clowning around. Every time my father went to parent's evening I would hear the car pull up to a skid and hear him shout,

'Where is he?'

Then I would get a good hiding for the embarrassment that he had just been forced to sit through, for being told his son was a clown and bottom of the class, yet another humiliating experience of my clowning about in the classroom. On another occasion my father was driving home and his mate said,

'Look at those thugs fighting in the park,' and as they looked my father saw it was me. I'd organised a fight between my class and the class opposite. In my eyes this was a personal achievement, but unfortunately not in my father's. When I arrived home I received another good hiding. Even though I was a rascal at the furthest stretch of the word I had a good childhood and spent most of my time fishing and shooting. These hobbies kept me and my mate busy from first to last light. If we weren't supposed to be there you could guarantee we probably were: any forbidden territories we would find them and if you had told us about them it was your own fault for telling us. I joined cubs and was made the pack sixer and even at an early age would organise games of football between the local village and the lads on the Royal Air Force camp I grew up on, so I do believe that the leader in me was always there, even as a young lad. I still have a trophy from the football match I organised: it makes me smile when I look at it as it has a big dent in it from where I shot it with my air rifle. We lived on an RAF base as my father was in the Air Force and one time we decided it would be a good idea to shoot the windows in the empty quarters. My mate's dad was the station officer. Unfortunately we got caught and the crime ended up in front of the station officer, who at this stage did not know it was his son who had done it. The station officer yelled at his Warrant Officer,

'I want the individual punished, and most of all I want his father put in front of me so I can sort him out!'

The Warrant replied,

'We have a problem sir; it's your son, and you are the father…'

I also had something built in me that would not allow anyone to think they were better than I was, and I would fight until I had no breath left in me to prove that I was as good or better than they were. I would constantly be outside the headmaster's office, normally for fighting with the year above us. We even had our desk attached to the teacher's so she could keep a close eye on us. I knew that being a soldier was for me as far back as I could remember, all that I had ever wanted to do was to join the Army. At the age of five somebody asked me what I wanted to do when I grew up, and I replied,

'I want to be a soldier.'

I was only interested in anything to do with the military; I collected medals and equipment from the Second World War and from the age of fifteen used to walk around in an army camouflage jacket. My family had a long history of military service: my father was an officer in the Royal Air Force and had served in Borneo, Brunei, Malaya and Northern Ireland, as was his father who was a Lancaster Rear Gunner in the Second World War. In the First World War members of the family served in the Army and Navy with two of them losing their lives, so the military was in my genes. My older brother had also joined the Army three years earlier.

I remember at school a soldier coming to visit us who had just come back from Northern Ireland, and I was in awe of him standing there in his uniform. He told us stories of how they were constantly shot at and how the children threw rocks at them whilst they were on patrol. He told us that he was on patrol and as he drove under a bridge the Irish dropped a brick on his head. He had to spend a week in hospital to get over his injuries. I just listened to him thinking, I want some of that. My mate's brother came home on leave from Ireland with his face beaten up. He told us that on patrol the Irish had tried pulling him out of his vehicle; there were three of them hitting him over his head with clubs, trying to take his weapon off him, but he managed to drive off and get away from them. I asked him why didn't he shoot them and he replied, 'If I had I would probably be in prison for murder now. There are times you can shoot and times you couldn't.' As I looked as his face that was in a right mess I thought that must have been enough reason to shoot them. Later on at school the Royal Marine Band came and did a concert and I thought it was amazing watching them in their best uniforms and playing military music. What I lacked in intelligence I made up in the desire to do something that I was quite obsessed with.

I had two lucky escapes as a child. The first one was when we decided to build a bike from old parts that we found at a scrap yard. We chose to test it out down the steepest hill around, and of course I volunteered to test it out first. The only problem was that we never got around to fitting brakes on it. I was found lying unconscious at the bottom of the hill as my head had taken the full impact of me falling off the bike, and had to spend a few days in hospital. The other was when a car crashed in to our car at seventy miles an hour. Luckily I was sitting on the side of the car that did not take the full impact and just got glass in my eyes. The driver of the car that hit us tried to apologise to my father, but my father was not interested. He gave him five seconds to get away from us as the man had nearly killed his son, so he ran off quickly.

I went off to the recruiting office without telling my parents, I'm not sure why I did not tell them, maybe I thought well, if I fail the test I would not have to go through the embarrassment of admitting I hadn't passed. I found myself walking up and down a steep hill in Lincoln (the hill is called Steep Hill so that tells you how steep it was), trying to pluck up the courage to enter the Recruiting Office. I was really scared about going in, I must have walked past the office about fifty times until I finally plucked up the courage, and I was met by a Recruiting Sergeant who said,

'What do you want, lad?'

I probably looked a bit of a mess, my face felt bright red and sweat pouring down me from constantly walking up and down the hill. I told him I wanted to join up and soon found myself at a desk in a small room sitting some exams. There were about five exams, Maths, English and some common sense ones which were designed to see if you were a total idiot or not. After about fifty minutes of exams that I did not find extremely hard, I found myself sitting in front of the Sergeant. I remember looking at his uniform and his stripes and thinking, I want some of them. I sat there nervously with him marking my papers. He was constantly shaking his head muttering under his breath,

'What do they teach them at school nowadays?'

It was a terrible feeling sitting there thinking that I had messed the papers up and could have failed. That would have been the end of my dream. He called his mate over who started shaking his head, grumbling,

'Dear oh dear, what are they sending us nowadays?'

At this stage I thought oh shit, how I am going to explain to everyone how I failed my test? I just decided that I wouldn't tell anyone and that would be the end of that. He then looked up and said,

'Well done, son! You have passed the first stage!'

I can't explain the relief I felt when he said these words, it's a bit like waiting to be told if you've passed your driving test or not.

'We sort out your medical and then your tests at Harrogate,' he continued. I was cursing him inside, it was obviously a game that he was playing with his mate to make me think I had failed the exams; it was my first taste of Army humour. I walked out of the office with my head held high, wanting to tell everyone that I was in the Army, although I did still have a few hurdles to pass before I was actually accepted.

The Army runs day to day with people constantly taking the piss out of each other, and not a day goes by where someone is not playing some sort of practical joke on some poor victim, many of whom are mentioned in this book. Mostly it was taken in the manner in which it was meant; of course sometimes people over-stepped the mark and it went into bullying. I can say that nowadays bullying is not accepted, but when I joined in the eighties it was rife. This was also my first taste of Army exams, which I probably spent at least three years on in total. I had lots of courses too. The Army is a lot more technical than some people realise. The qualifications you need to get promoted and make it up the ladder are quite hard. These days the Army is small and professional, not like the days of conscription where all you had to learn was to how to shoot and use a bayonet.

That day I was on top of the world telling all my friends and family that I had passed the Army test and I was going to be a soldier when I left school. As I hadn't told my mum and dad I was going to take my test, they were shocked and proud when I told them I had passed. I think they had been a bit worried that I was going to be a waster so this was good news to them that I had made the first step to doing something with my life. A few weeks later I had to go for my medical which was at the top of that bloody hill again, past the recruiting office. I walked in with the bright red face and sweat pouring down me again. I knew the doctor was going to grab my balls and make me cough, but it was a big shock when he asked me to bend down, and looked up my rear end … apparently to see if I had been interfered with. My first thought was, I hope I have cleaned it properly, my second was, I hope I don't fart in his face. Well I passed that hurdle with no farting and my bum must have been clean as he did not collapse. I later found out, however, that the doctor died three weeks later, I hoped it was nothing to do with the sight of my ring piece. I think it was due to the fact that he had to walk up and down that bloody hill every day. The medical is strict as you are going into a physical environment. A lot of lads failed at this stage.

About three months later I went to Harrogate and spent three more days on exams and completing a fitness test. When they put the maths paper down in front of me I opened it and saw the answers had been rubbed out. My first thought was that it was a trick as I could still make the figures out. I checked the first few, thought they looked good so I filled all one hundred questions in by going over what had already been written. I could not believe my good fortune. The papers were in the back office being marked, as I was doing the English paper I heard a voice say,

'Bloody hell have you seen this bloke, he has scored one hundred percent! He should be a brain surgeon, not be coming here!'

We spent three days doing tests, briefings, interviews and fitness tests, I didn't find this particularly strenuous but I am known for being modest about my strength, I tell people I'm a Spartan. A number of lads did fail, but that's the way the cookie crumbles. Contrary to belief the Army does not accept anyone; you have to be of a certain standard.

It was the first experience of being away from home for a lot of people and this made them throw their cards in when they realised they were homesick and did not want to join the Army. When I went for my final interview, the officer said I had done fantastically well on my exams, especially the maths paper. I replied by saying,

'I've been doing a lot of extra work and studying over the last few months, especially doing maths sums.'

I wonder what he would have done if he knew that I had been given a paper with the answers in. He asked a lot of questions and was really impressed that I had county trials at rugby and had done well at the fitness test. He asked me if I minded going to Northern Ireland, I thought to myself I was definitely in the wrong place if I did mind, and answered appropriately. He continued to say,

'Well done, you're in!'

He told me that I had a guaranteed place as a Junior Leader. In those days out of every ten who applied to be a Junior Leader only one was selected. I wanted to join the Parachute Regiment and then the Green Jackets; my third choice was the Royal Artillery because my brother was in it. Due to the fact that I would have had to wait a year extra to join the first two I was told that the Gunners were the Regiment for me, so that was where I was put. There were a lot of young lads who had not been accepted and were reduced to tears. I thought to myself how lucky I was not to be in their position.

The last thing I had to do was to go and take my oath, this is where you swear on the bible to defend your Queen and country and you get paid the Queen's shilling. Due to inflation it was no longer a shilling, it was a fiver. It must be about fifty pounds now. The feeling of going home and telling everyone the good news was amazing. At the age of fifteen years and four months I had guaranteed my place in the British Army. I felt so proud. The only problem was that I had about nine months left at school! Because I knew I was in the Army I just messed around even more than usual and did very little schooling. The only thing that slightly interested me was 'O'-level History and this was because you learnt about Northern Ireland. Those nine months went very slowly. After school ended I worked on a farm for four months, picking potatoes mainly, and generally just messed around with my mates for the rest of the time. Eventually, the day came when I was off to join the British Army.

It was 22 September 1981. I was now five foot seven, weighing eight and half stone, aged sixteen years and two months, and was off to join the Army, ready to do my bit for Queen and country.

I had a new suitcase and five pounds in my pocket. I got on the train and at every stop there were young lads doing the same, all of us going to the same place. Once we arrived at our destination we were met by two

Sergeants and taken to the camp, an old RAF base. We were taken to the gym where there must have been about four hundred of us all waiting to be told what to do next. We waited until our names were called out and went to the Troop Sergeant who was to be in charge of us for the next year. I was filled with excitement but was extremely nervous as well.

I spent one year at the Junior Leaders, which was where you did all the things that you do to turn you into a soldier, ready to go and join your regiment. You can imagine how thorough and strict these training establishments were, considering that within six months of leaving you could find yourself fighting in some conflict in another country. I do not think people realise how young soldiers are and how much responsibility they are given. When I first went to war I was twenty five, in charge of twelve men who had an average age of twenty.

I will just mention a few of the things that stand out during this year, most to do with some sort of violence. I must point out that bullying nowadays is not accepted in the Army and there is no place for it. The bullying is stopped and the bullies are punished.

At the Junior Leaders you spend the whole year doing fitness, soldiering and education; they say that thugs should have to go through this instead of prison. In my opinion they would not be able to handle the discipline and the respect that is required to make a good soldier. It is an honour to be in the Army and there is no place for people who don't want to work extremely hard as a team as well as an individual within a team. It is important to remember that the Army is in the business of killing or being killed, so the man next to you, who might one day make the difference from you living or dying, needs to be of high calibre too.

During the year you have a large Inter Troop Competition; they compete in drill, sports and military skills. It is the main event where the Troop Sergeants can compete and show off how talented their soldiers are. It also looks good on their report if they had the year's Champion Troop. The only problem was that the teams were picked by the Adjutant at random. They pick the names from each troop's nominal roll. I was picked to do the cross country run which was no problem to me. Troop Sergeants could not put their best people in the event of their choice, and had to rely on the luck of the draw. The reason it is done this way is to test the whole standard of the troop and not the case of putting the stars in certain events. Our Sergeant was mainly concerned about the Assault Course race. He was particularly interested in this event as he had been shot by the Irish Republican Army in the stomach whilst helping another soldier to climb a wall; this gave him a thing about being fit to get over walls, etc. His previous troop had won this event the year before and he was keen to keep the trophy. When he saw the team who had been picked he was not happy because the biggest, most unfit member of the Troop had been chosen. He knew that the Troop could not win the race and the fat lad knew this as well. The only way this could happen was if the chunky boy was ill or injured, and then the nominated reserve could take his place. That night the fat lad volunteered to have his fingers broken, this was his idea and it would not have happened unless he suggested it. The first idea he had was to put his fingers in the door frame while someone else shut the door hard. This was attempted four times with each time the lad screaming in pain, but his fingers were not broken (there was a lot of bleeding but that was it). The second was to use an old metal bed

14

end and strike his fingers with it like a sledgehammer hitting a wall, on this occasion it worked and the lad's fingers were broken. He screamed with pain and he went off to the Medical Centre to get medical attention and pretended he had had an accident. In my opinion he should have been nominated for a bravery award. There was no way I could have done that. The Troop Sergeant said he had had an accident as this was what the lad told him, the reserve was put in and the team won. This is a great example how it is not your Queen and country you fight for but the team you are in. He did not want to let his team down and as he knew that the team could not win with him in it he did what he thought was necessary. This could be classed as bullying but I point out the lad came up with the idea and I think he thought that having to do the assault course would have caused him more pain than having his fingers broken. He was extremely unfit and suffered every time we had to do cardiovascular exercise.

The British Army works on teams and teams within the big team, so all over the battlefield you have people not wanting to let each other down. This I believe is why the British Army is so good. The country has a part to play and in some cases the Queen bit, but the main part is the team and not wanting to let your comrades down. I always remember the Troop Sergeant as a big strong figure, but in those days I was only sixteen and weighing eight and half stone so he would have looked like a giant. I met him twenty years later when I was an RSM; he looked like a frail, little old man. It's funny how people and places always look bigger when you are younger.

Due to many reasons we lost a lot of soldiers during the year, some just were homesick, some injured, some quit and some were just not fit enough and they were kicked out. The ones that realised pretty quickly that they had made a massive mistake left at the first opportunity. It is hard going in to an environment full of young keen men where the training is difficult mentally and physically. You are constantly pushed to your limits, as well as being away from home with very little money or social life. Back home your mates are out every night doing what sixteen year olds do, while you find yourself spending hours doing your kit for the inspection for the next day. The strange thing is when you go home on leave and you realise how much you have changed from the way your mates are. You change mentally and of course physically as doing PT every day does change your body. There were lots of Dear John letters where the girlfriends were not willing to wait for their man to return. I saw a lot of strong, fit, confident men break down and cry like babies on the receipt of these letters as their girlfriends back home were giving them a focus point to get through the hard training.

We had to go to church every Sunday, which was obligatory. I hated it. The officers had to be seen as regular church goers, even if they did not believe in God. This was most of us soldiers, but you still had to go and pretend that you believed there was a little man up there, sitting on the clouds, wishing us all good. Every Sunday you were marched to the church in your best suit. In my case it was a hand me down from my older brother (in fact I think most of the soldiers were dressed in hand me downs). On one occasion after the service the Junior Troop Sergeant started screaming his head off. He said that we had not been singing loudly enough. I had always believed you never let anyone talk to you threateningly and you should always stand up for yourself. Even if you lose you must let them know that they have been in a battle, this I believe stops them from starting on you again. I was a quiet lad who did not mouth it off, but I was not scared of anyone and knew that I could look after myself. I found through my career, especially amongst the officers, that they judge someone by their appearance. If you are big and shout a lot, it gives the impression that you are hard, but this is often not the case. Some of the strongest, hardest lads I have come across have been the ones who look least like it. Most of them were nice lads because they knew they didn't have to be loud and act the hard man, having said this, if they lost it, then you knew about it.

We were on parade at the stand at ease position with our hands behind our back; the Junior Sergeant then said he was going to beat us. I thought he was a bully and wasn't too good at being quiet, so said to him,

'Don't think so,' and looked to the side. As I turned back around the Junior Troop Sergeant had head butted me and punched me three times, splitting my lip, chipping my tooth and just to top it off he'd also given me a black eye. As I was on parade and in the standing at ease position with my hands behind my back, I could not defend myself. In response without giving it too much thought I'd punched him back, and the fight was stopped by the Troop Sergeant. I was really frustrated because he'd attacked me with my hands behind my back and I couldn't let it lie. We were marched back to the accommodation block, me with blood running down my face and very angry. In my opinion he had been a coward because he had attacked me when my hands were behind my back. On the order 'fall out' I ran over to him and punched him again but once more the sergeants broke it up. We were then ordered to get in our PT kit so we could go to the gym and sort it out in the boxing ring.

17

(This is what happened when soldiers had disputes. They would be put in the boxing ring and you would fight until one of you could not go on.) I wanted to fight him in the toilets as he was a boxer and I knew I had more of a chance doing it my way. I was so angry that he had attacked me in front of everyone when I couldn't defend myself, and I knew that given the chance, one on one in the toilets, I could put up a good showing. The only way he would stop me then would have been if he knocked me out, even though when I recovered I would have had another go. I was not going to be an easy victim. The sergeants didn't want their blue-eyed boy defeated or even anyone standing up to him, and I think this was the first time anyone had even tried to do so, and they did not like it. Fortunately it was all sorted out with there being no more violence. Everyone was coming up to me saying it was about time someone stuck up to him, this made me feel proud of what I'd done in front of my mates. He even came up to me and said,

'Sorry, you scared me, because no-one's ever challenged me before now.'

I must admit I hadn't been singing in church, and did deserve to be told off, but not in the way he thought appropriate. I did not believe in God and didn't like pretending you were something you were not. Religion wasn't my thing and still isn't.

On parade the next day the Battery Commander (BC) who was inspecting our Troop asked me what I had done to my face. I said a cricket ball had caught me whilst playing. He knew I was lying but did not ask any more questions and the Troop Sergeant looked at me and winked as if to say well done for not saying anything. It's all about being a man and accepting that things like that happen now and again: it was taken in the heat of the moment.

About twenty years later when we were Regimental Sergeant Majors, I met the Junior Troop Sergeant and he told me that I had changed his life. This is what he said:

'No-one had stuck up to me before, I realised what a twat I'd been.'

I agreed he was a twat, we had a beer and laughed about it.

Another incident I experienced unfortunately was my first meeting with military law. We were in the Isle of Man, Adventure Training for the week. We were on a trip to the local town on the back of a military truck. I had just enjoyed my food and hastily I threw my rubbish in to an empty cardboard box at the back of the vehicle; unfortunately for me it missed and fell in the road. Little did I know some idiot earlier had chucked theirs into a local's garden. The resident had complained to the camp and obviously because of my poor aim I was blamed for the idiot's dirty habits. As a punishment I was put on Battery Commander's orders and was given five days' restriction of privileges. I had to go and sleep on a hill-top, acting as the pit stop for hikers, making brews, etc. It made me really mad. I got five days' punishment for chucking a sandwich out of a vehicle because of someone else's crime. I was sentenced under Section 69, 'Bringing the Army into Disrepute'. If they cannot find a crime in the military law book, then they use section 69, which covers everything.

It was a frightening experience being marched in front of the Battery Commander. I was marched in front of him twice as the first time I messed up my drill, got screamed at and had to do it again. You felt you were up for murder with all sorts of people shouting at you and calling you a twat. In my later service as a Warrant Officer I had a lot of dealings with military law where I was the man doing the shouting and some poor victim was on the receiving end. I will mention them later on.

Using your sporting talents to your advantage was something I learnt early in my career. If you are a good sportsman it can help you immensely, mainly due to the fact it gets your face known by the sergeants and officers. I was lucky and could do most sports at a good level. They wanted me to represent the Regiment at rugby and squash, but I didn't want to do both as I wanted to concentrate fully on squash at the time. The Battery Commander at the time had been blown up by the IRA, and as he was a keen rugby man I was marched straight into his office (I seemed to be surrounded by victims of the Ireland conflict). He said to me,

'If you don't play rugby I will send you to a Regiment that you do not want to go to. If you do as I say your life will be a lot easier.'

'I want to play squash,' I replied, and all I remember was him screaming at me and sending me out of his office. My Troop Sergeant called me a twat and marched me about the drill square for a while and no more was said. The BC was true to his word and sent me where I did not want to go to. I wanted to go to a Field Gun Regiment in England; he sent me to a Missile Regiment in Germany.

I found during my career that the officer comes in one of the three following categories. The first one is the extremely efficient, clever, and excellent leader. The second is the complete 'nasty bastard' who cares about nothing apart from his career; he will shit on anyone who gets in the way of his plans. The third is the young officer who is Jack the lad and good fun but really does not know much about soldiering. He has about seven years' experience, then he goes down the route of the first two examples, or he leaves the Army. Later on in my career I had to work in headquarters where the brightest officers work. I must say I was most impressed by their coolness and intelligence. From colonel onwards they are very bright men indeed. During my career I met a lot of great officers, some of whom I am friends with to this day, but I also met a lot of bad ones who made every soldier under their command's life a misery. I am glad to say that an officer cannot just join nowadays as a result of his class and influence, such as was the case in years gone by, with terrible results, poor leadership and thousands of lives lost. I know that in certain regiments it helps if you have the right connections and money, but on the whole they are selected on merit.

The year ended with a massive passing out parade where all the families came to watch us march around the parade square in our best uniforms; it was a very proud moment for us and for them. To be on the parade square in your best uniform with the band playing made the whole year worth it.

We were sent to Woolwich in London for another twelve week course of training before we were posted to our regiments. This was because Woolwich was a training camp for older recruits and they were not busy due to a lack of recruits at the time so it was decided that our intake should go there to keep them occupied and to give us some extra training.

It was a nightmare. We were Junior Leaders, and not people straight off the streets, and the training staff gave us hell in an attempt to show that their training establishment was harder than the one we had just come from. You find this a lot in the Army units, people always trying to prove they are better than the others. It is a good thing in some respects, as soldiers take pride in their unit and want to be the best. Before we had got to our units we had completed sixteen months of training.

Whilst at Woolwich I had my first experience of boxing. There was to be an Inter Troop Boxing competition. The way they picked the team for the Troop was to put you in a line, with the tallest on the right, working all the way down to the smallest on the left. They then paired you off with the person next to you, and you then hit each other for two minutes. You have two options here. You can pretend you can't do it and get battered so you don't get picked for the team, or you can try your best. My pride got the better of me and I went for it. My first punch knocked my opponent's tooth out, so they put me in again with the biggest lad. We spent two minutes hitting each other; he was at least three stone heavier than I was but I held my own. My head hurt for days afterwards. That was it, I was in the team. You did not have a choice if you were picked: you did what you were told.

We spent about eight weeks training, up at five o'clock doing PT until seven, then work, followed by two more hours of PT and boxing skills at night. We had our medicals to make sure we were fit to box; this was the only chance you had to get out of it. If you told the doctor you did not want to fight, he would put you down as unfit to box due to medical reasons. I think a few people did take this option, can't really blame them, it takes a lot of courage to enter the ring and some people just have not got what it takes! Or you could just call me down right stupid. Fight night came and it was terrifying: there were at least seven hundred spectators all dressed up in their best uniforms, plus lots of important local people. The band played the national anthem and the fighting began. In the changing rooms I was shaking like a drug addict going cold turkey; they had trouble putting my bandages on my hands and I constantly needed the toilet. I don't know why but whenever I get nervous I need to go to the toilet every five minutes. It was not that I was scared of the opponent but I was scared of looking an idiot in front of all those people. All that kept going through my head was that I must not get knocked down and carried out on a stretcher. I ironed my kit really well so at least if I was carried out I looked the part. I think I was about the fifth to fight and as I waited in the changing room I could hear each fighter being introduced, the bell ring and a mass of cheering as though I was in a football crowd. After each fight I was thinking, 'Oh shit, my turn next!' Then it was time, my Troop Sergeant came in to the changing room and said,

'Ok, it's time!' I thought he could at least have come in and said it had been cancelled, but before I knew it I was being led into this packed gym with seven hundred people screaming and the band playing some sort of tune. I cannot remember much about the fight, it was all a bit of blur. It is really strange that whilst you are in the ring you cannot hear the crowd. We were introduced by the RSM and as our names were called we did a smart about turn and then faced our corner again. I remember my trainer saying,

'He looks handy!' I looked at him and said,

'Thanks for that, that makes me feel loads better.' He then realised his mistake and started a verbal round of encouragement in his broad Scottish accent. I think it was encouragement but I remember him saying, 'Sort yourself out or I beat you up before you start!' His mad verbal gabble was quite crazy; he was like a mad man who was going in the ring himself. I finally brought myself to and realised that this was it, so had to go for it. For three rounds we went toe to toe, he had two standing counts where I had hit him hard. I remember after the first round the Sergeant saying,

'What are you doing?'

'I haven't a clue,' I replied. I then spat my water into the bucket, but missed, and it went all over one of the judges.

'You stupid twat!' squealed my Sergeant, 'you've well and truly blown it now!'

When I got back in the ring I took my first blinder of a punch. He hit me and things went a little dizzy, but I had caught him at the same time so he got the standing count. I think he was pissed off because he knew he had caught me square. I realised at this stage that to box for three rounds at three minutes each, you had to be very fit. The fight came to an end and I was so pleased I was still standing. The next moment my hand was held in the air by the referee and I was told I was the winner. It didn't really sink in that I had won; we were marched out and led back to the changing room. I wasn't that bothered that I had won but was chuffed I had held my own and put on a good display. At the end of the night all the boxers were put in a line and all seven hundred spectators applauded us. The RSM called two of our names out, at first I did not reply because I thought they might want me to fight again and I really couldn't face another one, then my Troop Sergeant shouted,

'Get back in there you idiot, I'll bloody box you myself if you don't sort yourself out, you muppet!'

Before I knew it I was standing in the ring again with another lad. He was presented with the best loser award and I was presented with the best boxer of the night award. The man who presented us the trophies was a man named Woodcock, an ex British heavyweight champion. I still have the trophy and look at it with pride. I remember walking out thinking that I would never do that again, how wrong was I, if the Army finds out you have a talent then they use it, even if you don't want to.

When I joined my Regiment they had an Inter Battery Boxing Competition. The Sergeant in charge of finding a team came up to me and said,

'You are in the team.'

'I don't want to do it again,' I replied.

'Well,' he answered, 'if you don't, I'll box you myself, then put you in jail and the Battery Commander will make sure you don't have a career in the Army.'

So like this I was 'gently' persuaded to do it and the whole drama started again. It is all part of being a soldier: if ordered to do something, you do it. It's not a job where you can say that you'll think about it and get back to them, or you'll check with the union.

You are trained to do what you are told. Of course people will moan about certain things they have to do, but they will do it.

This was to be my first experience with a soldier who had shot at the IRA. He had been in a watch tower when a vehicle stopped and a man jumped out to throw a bomb at a target. This soldier was an alert young man and had fired at the men, stopping the attack.

When you have men living together the one thing that is not tolerated is thieving. On one occasion a lad had been caught stealing and hidden all of his stolen loot under the baths. He got the biggest kicking of his life by those he had stolen from. After his punishment he was marched to the guardroom for his own safety and was later kicked out of the Army. One thing I hate is thieves as it causes so much pain for the victims; the other thing I hate is those thugs who just chuck their rubbish on the floor, as often witnessed outside MacDonald's. Pure laziness and unnecessary.

My sergeant was a Commando and he wanted me and another lad to try for his Commando regiment. He gave us three days of just following him around to make the decision. I thought about it but concluded that life was fine whilst I was young but promotion would be easier in a regiment where there is no selection. I told him my decision and his reply was, 'You stay a crap hat then, you're wasting a talent!' Commandos and paras call normal regiments 'crap hats'.

When my time at Woolwich came to an end, I went to join my Regiment and after nearly a year and half of training was ready to start my career of soldiering. As I left training the Falklands conflict had just started. I heard a story about this war that I found particularly amazing, and which tells a lot about the British soldier. It was the last day in the Army for an SAS soldier and he was told he could not go with the rest of his unit to the conflict as he was due to become a civilian the next day. He decided he was going to put a different beret on and join another unit. This unit boarded the ship heading south the next day. He nearly got away with his plan until just before the ship sailed, when he was asked to report to the captain. The soldier found two military police waiting to escort him off the ship. To cut a long story short, his wife had phoned them and told them to get her extra special mad crazy twat of a husband off the ship and send him home.

Before I went to my new posting in Germany, I had three weeks' leave. On this particular leave two of my friends and I were driving along when another car came speeding over the top of the hill towards us. The driver lost control, skidded on to our side of the road and hit us at seventy miles per hour. It seemed to happen in slow motion. I was in the front passenger seat. I sat there and watched the engine slide about a foot into my lap, missing my vital organs by just a few inches. My mate in the back came flying into the front seat; I was winded and cut by the pressure of the seat belts to my body. I managed to fall out of the door and, still winded, was struggling to breathe. My mate in the back was lying on the ground, his back in agony, and my other mate had blood rushing from his face. He didn't seem to be stopping bleeding, he was losing a lot and it was quite scary. It took me about five minutes to breathe properly as my ribs were badly damaged. In anger, without thinking, I crawled to the car that had hit us to give the driver a slap but as I opened his door I saw he was out of it. Blood was spurting from his neck and arm. His leg was hanging off below the knee and was only attached by an inch of a muscle. I did some first aid on him, possibly saving his life, and about five minutes later the police arrived. I was put in an ambulance and spent the rest of my leave in bed with extremely painful ribs. I read the newspaper headlines about the accident and it said that a policeman had saved the man's life, the twat had taken the credit for what I had done!

Also I remember just before the accident I was walking along a high street and in front of me were some builders having a coffee break. I heard them singing, 'Walks like a poof!' to the tune of 'Walks like an Egyptian', which was in the charts at the time. They were doing it to every man that went by, but all I can say is I was slightly over reactive in those days (sometimes not much has changed as I still hate twats who start on innocent people). I walked on for about another hundred metres saying to myself, just to let it go, but then something inside said 'I am not having that,' and turned around and walked up to them again.

'Ok, which one first?' I asked the six of them. By rights at this stage I should have been battered but they were so shocked that this little man had offered them out and they all apologised to me. This was again me not letting people think they are better than I was. I was willing to fight to show them they should not take the piss out of strangers, they didn't know who I was and didn't know what I was capable of.

This reminds me of the saying, 'never judge a man till you have walked a mile in his shoes'.

CHAPTER TWO
Regiment

The kind-hearted Battery Commander who had said that if I did not play rugby he would send me to the Missile Regiment kept his word, and sent me to the regiment I wanted to be in the least. I was seventeen and half years old and was posted to Germany as part of the British Army of the Rhine. It was winter and there was snow everywhere. I found that in Germany you can have snow on the ground from November to March if it's a particularly bad winter. We got off the coach and were taken to our batteries. There were four of us and each one of us was allocated to a different battery. On the first night we were shown around by the Padre and the duty officer. We were the first new lads that the regiment had had for a long time. It is a very nerve-wracking experience joining a regiment for the first time. There are highly trained soldiers everywhere, whereas before you were surrounded by recruits of your own age and a few instructors who were looked upon as gods. Now you were surrounded by men and proper soldiers of all ages: you were their new toy and you were not sure what to do or even what to say. At the beginning of your soldiering you are just learning the basic skills and have to humble yourself and almost wait to be accepted.

Each battery had its own drinking establishments and the profits went back into the battery and were used to fund functions and improvements. We were taken on arrival to have one drink; it was like a scene from a western with some of the older soldiers in there staring at us, not making us feel very welcome, of course you would get men that ended up every night in these establishments but I would point out that it was the minority and not the majority of soldiers who did this. The only thing that was missing was someone playing on the piano. After our one drink we were told to leave the bar, and were told by the older members,

'Now sprogs, don't come back in here until you have served some time.'

We were then handed over to representatives of our batteries and shown to our rooms.

For the first six months some of the senior soldiers would treat you like their new toy. A regiment is made up of all sorts of characters, aged from seventeen to forty, some of them high flyers and some who were destined to go nowhere, some are polite and real gentlemen and some are rough thugs. They're from all walks of life, all with different backgrounds and from all over the country. The good thing about the Army it does not matter what and where you come from, it is what you do from the moment you join that counts. Everyone is given a chance to prove themselves and make it to the top. A lot of lads with deprived backgrounds do very well as they find something to belong to; a new family. I found that sometimes the more experienced soldiers were show offs and used their gained time in the Army as a weapon to feed their self importance; they could become bullies if given the chance and would take money off the youngsters. As a new boy it was important to be able to look after yourself, otherwise these types of men would eat you for breakfast. I found that the good ones wanted to look after you and it was a good idea to seek these out. I am pleased to say there are more good ones than bad and the bad are few in number but every organisation in the world has them. You normally find there are great Detachment Commanders, Corporals and Sergeants who take you under their wing and look after you. When I was a Battery Sergeant Major (BSM) and I heard Detachment Commanders moaning about the new lads. I used to say,

'Do you remember how you were when you first joined? It is your job to train them and turn them in to good soldiers, and most importantly look after them, especially out in the field on exercise, and especially on operational tours. It takes time and training and patience to get good at soldiering. You can't expect them to come out of training and be the finished article! When they reach their regiments is when that starts.'

Some people learn quickly, some are a bit slower. The truth was if they were rubbish then that often meant they were not being taught properly and the Detachment Commanders were rubbish teachers. If I found a soldier had not had his haircut or something like that I would have a word with his Detachment Commander and Troop Sergeant as well as the soldier, as it was those above him who should have sorted him out.

On my first day I was marched in front of my Battery Commander who read my reports from training. He read them and said,

'I think we bin the one from Junior Leaders which is rubbish, and keep the one from Woolwich which is good. I am going to pretend I have not read the first one and we go forward from your stay at Woolwich.'

My reports had the same theme, they said I had the capability to do well but was too quiet and did not show what I was capable of. I put this down to a lack of confidence, which took a while to develop, but the Army is very good at getting the best out of you and working on your weaker areas. If I was in large groups I found it hard to stand out and was quiet, I had to make an effort to get noticed. Lots of people were loud and confident and stood out sooner; a lot of these looked the part but lacked skills and common sense. Over time I showed that even though I wasn't loud I had a lot to say but liked to wait so when I did speak it was something worth listening to. When I look back I think fighting with the Junior Sergeant and the sandwich bouncing out of the vehicle had done me no favours, hence the rubbish report from Junior Leaders. Having said this, being the best boxer at Woolwich had given me an excellent write up. This I think re-enforces the theory that if your face fits and you have people above you who like you at the right time in your career, you strike lucky: this makes all the difference between making it to the top or not. I marched out of the Battery Commander's Office and decided that this was the stage of my life where I was going to do well.

I was put in a room which was next door to the Lance Bombardier who had just been killed by the IRA. He had been on patrol in Belfast and was searching a block of flats where the IRA had left a bomb in a drain pipe which exploded next to him, killing him; I think he was nineteen years old. Such a young age to give your life to your country. I watched as his belongings were put in to a box to be sent home to his grieving parents. He had been at the Junior Leaders two intakes before I had joined.

That night I lay in bed wondering what was in store for me on my first day at work the next day. I heard some shouting in the corridor and heard the words,

'Let's get the new sprog, I think he lives in here!'

My door was kicked open and three drunken Gunners who had served in the Regiment for years came in and shouted,

'Sprog, Bratwurst and chips, now!'

It was my first day and I didn't want any trouble so I climbed out of bed, got dressed and said,

'Where's the shop?'

They told me it was directly outside the camp.

'Can I have your money to get your food?' I continued.

'Don't you understand, sprog?' they replied, 'you get it, and pay for it, and you do it every night until we tell you to stop!'

It was one of those moments in life where you have to stand up for yourself or you're going to be used over and over, so I replied,

'Sorry I am not doing that. But I don't want any trouble.' With that, three of them attacked me shouting,

'You're lippy for a sprog, who do you think you are?'

I got some good punches in. My dad had always taught me not to start hitting people who are causing trouble, it does no good, but if you put your fingers in their eyes, kick their shins and stand on their toes, it puts them out of action, then you can hit them and it might work. I was lucky this night because they were so pissed they couldn't control their arms and legs properly. The Flat Bombardier, one of the good guys, heard the racket and came in, broke the fight up and got rid of the drunks. I was standing there with not a mark on me and they looked as though they had been in a battle. He said,

'Well done sprog, for sticking up for yourself. You won't get no more trouble from them, if you do I think you'll be ok to sort them out yourself.'

He explained they were just wasters and he would sort them out in the morning. In those days people could stay in the Army for twenty two years and remain a private, so you can imagine some of the thugs you had just cruising along with no intention of exerting themselves and no ambition. They were just doing enough to get by. In later years the Army got very strict and if you did not make a certain rank in a certain amount of time they would send you a brown envelope saying your services are no longer required. This sometimes did not work as a good thing because a lot of good soldiers got kicked out as they were not going to make it to a certain rank. Some of these were good at what they did so it was a waste of an asset.

The next nine months went quietly. I did find a way to get out of the regiment and get to a field regiment in England; I managed to get my older brother to claim me to his regiment. The Army has a system where an older member can claim a younger member of his family to serve with him. This I did and I escaped the sentence that the Battery Commander had put on me for not playing Rugby (a small victory). I have always seemed to have found a way to beat someone who has tried to get one over on me.

Whist I was in Germany I had my first experience of true pain and how hard soldiering can be. This was due to the severe cold of the German winter, and after my experience I will never understand how the Germans survived on the eastern front in the Second World War in similarly arctic conditions, poorly clothed and hungry. I can understand now the stories you hear that it was so cold that some soldiers just wandered off and shot themselves because they could not take the pain of being cold and starving any more.

The Army uniform that we were issued was very poor as far as keeping you warm and dry were concerned.

You were issued waterproofs that we called crisp packets (that's about how much use they were; they did not keep you dry). Your boots were made from compressed cardboard and they would freeze solid once wet; they did not keep your feet even comfy let alone dry. The sleeping bags were useless as they had about two feathers in and were designed for men who were four foot four. You had webbing and a large pack to carry your equipment and ammunition, but as this was the size of a school bag you could not fit anything in. We still had putties wrapped around the top of the boots like the ones you see in the war films and the old type of helmets that had a metal spike in that stuck in your head. The uniform had not improved since the end of the war. Soldiers used to buy better equipment to wear on exercise to make the experience more comfortable but it was extremely expensive and I was too tight to fork out the cash: in those days I did not have the money to afford them. I deployed on exercise with the basic uniform, with temperatures of minus seventeen and in the pouring rain. It is not until you have been in that environment that you can really understood how unforgiving nature can be. It was so cold and so painful that I had to volunteer for every patrol to keep moving. It is really one of those things that you cannot understand unless you have been through that much discomfort. If you can imagine all your kit being wet then freezing and then standing in the middle of the night in a trench with no sleep then you might get some idea. I learnt a valuable lesson, once wet you have had it as far as keeping yourself warm. You can have the best equipment to wear but if it is wet it is useless. I learnt that you must stay dry and if you couldn't do that, at least have dry good quality equipment to put on once you had the chance to change. With one hour's sleep a night you end up as though you are drunk. Your boots froze at night and if you took them off you had great trouble getting them back on. I kept thinking that I only did five days of it … I can't imagine how those poor soldiers went through on the eastern front in the Second World War for months on end, it is absolutely horrid and it takes all your effort to carry out just your every day tasks. Soldiering was at its worst in those conditions. In the nineties a lot of money was put into the soldier's kit and it was fantastic. It kept you warm and dry and each soldier's uniform was worth about five thousand pounds. It really annoyed me when I heard that the younger soldiers complained about it, they had no idea how bad it used to be.

It was on this exercise that one of the vehicles carrying eighteen men in the back of it had an accident, three men were killed and lots injured. People do not realise how many soldiers are killed on training exercises.

Whilst in Germany I had a chance to be part of a launcher crew to fire a nuclear missile into the North Sea from the Hebrides in Scotland. As you can imagine, firing one of these missiles is a major event. The missile itself cost millions and it cost the tax payer a lot of money to fly the unit over to Scotland to fire it. Each crew got the chance to fire one of these multi-million pound missiles once a year; you would spend months training for the big day. My job was the fin man, I had to fit these big fins to the missile body and do a few other small jobs; the fins were my big part in the firing of the missile. We drove on to the firing site with hundreds of spectators watching from a safe distance. Everyone started running around doing their individual jobs. We used to have to wear the full individual protection clothing which was a suit made from charcoal, a gas mask and gloves that were either to small you could not get your hands in or so big you looked like Coco the Clown. On this day I had the Coco the Clown version. I took the fins out of the box, which were about one metre long and three feet wide, placed them on the missile and secured them into the lugs that held them in place. Then the finger from my glove got caught inbetween the fin and the missile body, and as I pulled away, the finger of the glove ripped off and was left dangling there. I panicked but did not want to tell anyone as we had so many spectators. I knew everyone would take the piss if the firing had to stop due to my Coco the Clown finger having to be removed from the missile; I decided not to say anything and carried on as normal. We all retired to the firing point, an old armoured car situated one hundred metres away from the missile. As I stood there I kept saying to myself, shit, shit, shit, I had visions of the missile flying all over the place due to the finger of my glove being stuck in the fin, or worse, even blow the whole thing up! I remember thinking if I got five days' restriction of privileges for throwing a sandwich out of a vehicle which I did not do I would probably get shot for this cock up. My Sergeant looked through his binoculars to see if everything on the missile was ok. He then said,

'Oh my god, no I don't believe it!' He then looked at me and took another look at the missile, then turned back to me,

'Please tell me that the thing dangling from the missile fin is not your missing finger from your glove? Let me look at your hand!' As I bought my hand out from behind my back, I apprehensively whispered,

'Yes Sergeant, I've fucked up!'

'You twat!' was his reply.

The countdown began; it was the longest ten seconds of my life. TEN, NINE, EIGHT, SEVEN, SIX, ... FOUR (they always miss out 'five' in case is it is mistaken as 'fire') THREE, TWO, ONE, FIRE! On that command a button was pressed and the missile was supposed to fire. There was a short delay but then the missile shot into the air, heading out to the North Sea, it was out of sight in seconds. I spent the next three minutes waiting for someone to come down and tell us the missile had gone all over the place, and I was in the shit with the boss, but all was well and it landed where it should have done, seventy kilometres away from us in the North Sea. I must point out here that the missile was fitted with a concrete warhead and not the real nuclear warhead.

My father told me that when he was stationed in the Christmas Islands in the sixties he was one of the servicemen who had to go and watch the atom bomb being dropped to see if it had any effects on them. He did go grey at the age of twenty. It's strange that thirty years later I would be part of a crew that could fire a nuclear warhead. My father told me that whilst he was there he was stationed with some soldiers. One of them was a Staff Sergeant who kept giving his lads a hard time for being lazy. A Lance Corporal had enough one day a decided to stand up to the Staff Sergeant. They both went outside the accommodation to have a fight. The Lance Corporal said, 'I am not fighting you with your shirt and rank on.' With that, the Staff Sergeant took his shirt off and said, 'Come on then.' The Lance Corporal picked the shirt up, screwed it up and rubbed it in the dirt, then ran off shouting, 'Have some of that you knob!' leaving the Staff Sergeant standing there, red faced.

On one particular exercise we were acting as an enemy for the Black Watch, and they were being an enemy against our unit. During the exercise the Black Watch had been attacked by some of our lads and had taken a beating, so unfortunately they were after revenge. We had to guard our missiles and on one occasion were told that the Black Watch were on their way to attack us. The Battery Sergeant Major stood there with a pick axe and shouted,

'Not one of them gets past me!' I was eighteen and was standing there waiting to defend the site for when the attack happened. Suddenly there were about forty screaming Jocks attacking us, it was as though it was a real war but without the bullets and people actually dying. There were pitched battles going on everywhere, and the umpires whose job it was to make sure everything was done safely lost control of the situation. A Jock came running up to me and shouted,

'You seen the films, you read the books now experience the real thing!'

With that I hit him across the legs with a pick axe. He fell down and I whispered in his ear,

'Now experience my mate Peter Pick-axe!' and left him hobbling about. The Battery Sergeant Major saw this and smiled at me. At the same time he was chasing one of them, waving his own pick-axe. It showed me what it is like to be on the receiving end of British troops when they revved up, it's not a pretty sight. I can see why we normally kick arse when war comes along. It all comes down to being proud of your unit and your team, It was funny watching a young Jock being tossed on the perimeter barbed wire, the rest of them running over him so they could get over the obstacle. He just laid there whilst all the other Jocks were running over him, screaming as they got inside our perimeter, to be met by us with our pick-axes.

We had American equipment in Germany so had to have some Americans attached to us. They controlled the warheads to the missiles, and they were the only ones who held the codes to arm them. Where we have six men to do a job they have twelve; the British Army is smaller but we are better trained with lots of individuals knowing and doing different tasks. They had one man who did one task and that was it. It used to take the Americans twelve minutes to bring the missile into action, whereas it took us about five, with half the amount of men that the Americans used. One of the Americans had fought in the Vietnam War; he would not talk about it but slept with his knife under his pillow every night as he was still being scared after what he had been through over there. In my opinion the American soldiers were not as professional, but they did not have to be as their army is so much bigger than ours. The Americans carried a card which said on it, don't fight, drink or gamble with the British soldier: you will probably lose.

My next posting was to the Field Regiment of my choice at Colchester, England. I had spent eleven months in Germany and in my opinion it was a total waste of time and had put me back eleven months in the promotion race. The BSM would not sign my clearance chit in the Missile Regiment unless I brought £20 of raffle tickets. I did this willingly as I was desperate to get away from there. Firing one missile a year was not for me. Being part of a gun crew where you were firing and in action all year around was where I wanted to be. I arrived at my new camp in Colchester and reported to the Guardroom at my new Regiment. I was met by the Provost Sergeant who was sitting at his desk. I told him who I was and he replied with,

'Have you ever seen anything like this before?'

'Like what?' I asked. I didn't know what he was on about.

He stood up.

'This, man!' and I was introduced to a nine-inch long manhood. I had never seen anything like it before, obviously! He had a big smile on his face, bragging. 'Very impressive, hey?'

'Yes, it is,' I replied. What else could I say?

That seemed to be what he wanted to hear and he directed me to my new Battery Office (still with his lengthy manhood dangling between his legs). Apparently he was really proud of his enormous dick and liked to show it off at every opportunity. I walked off, thinking, that was strange – what is in store for me next? That night was the Battery Christmas Function before they deployed to the Falklands on a six month tour, it was a great night, everyone was friendly and I had a great time. It was totally different from my experience of when I first joined the missile regiment. It helped having my brother in the same unit and the fact I had served a year in another regiment, so I was not a sprog straight out of training.

On return to my room I was met by a body being thrown down the steps, shortly followed by two others. Then this huge man jumped on all three of them and gave them a good kicking. I later found out he was the Battery Sergeant Major; he had a chest the size of a house, and apparently was as hard as one. I found out later the three soldiers had got drunk and had mouthed it off to him, so he had educated them the best way he knew. In those days a soldier would often prefer a beating or a couple of punches rather than having to go on orders where you could have lots of money taken off you, or even be sent to jail. Battery Sergeant Majors would often say, 'Do you accept my punishment? Or do you want to go on orders for your crime?' Of course the soldier would take his punishment. This meant you might have sore ribs for a few days where you had been punched a couple of times but not a record. A few of the lads thought I was new boy from training and didn't realise I had spent a year in another regiment and tried it on, but I was a lot wiser now, plus my brother was in the battery so this of course helped me to get settled in and accepted.

Colchester was a great posting, especially if you were single. There were hundreds of girls and every weekend there was one walking about the accommodation from the night before. Some of these girls were a bit rough, though. I remember one of them used to like the soldier in question to wear a motorbike helmet and head butt her whilst they were having sex. My mate would never go out as when he got drunk he would end up with her. One night he did and when I awoke in the morning I looked over to his bed and he was looking at me as to say, 'Oh shit, I done it again!' There was the woman in his bed with him and the motorcycle helmet was on the floor. Some of the rooms used to have four soldiers sleeping in them and on one occasion two of the lads brought back four girls, two of whom were for their mates who had not gone out that night. One of the girls went over to one of the soldiers, who was lying in his bed and asked him if there was anything she could do for him (the other three were all having sex). He replied,

'Actually yes, could you sew a button on to my trousers?'

Everyone burst out laughing and the girl stormed out in a huff, the lad had the piss taken out of him for years and was forever asked if he needed anything doing for him.

During the year I spent ten weeks on courses learning gunnery, the equipment I was on was now the FH-70 155mm towed howitzer, a totally different type of artillery equipment to that which I had trained on before. Another soldier was killed on one of our many training exercises. He was air sentry on one of the limber vehicles when it overturned and crushed him to death. His mates had to clean the vehicle up which was covered in the dead soldier's body parts. There were lots of accidents on exercise. One of the loaders of the gun crew caught his finger in the loading tray and took the top of it off, the crew stuck it in a matchbox, had a good laugh about him and the finger and packed them both off to the hospital. The commander of the gun shouted,

'Get fingers out of here and get me someone in here to load the shell!' That was how people in the Army coped with everything; they made a joke out of it and cracked on. If someone was injured you got medical help but cracked on with the job you had to do. I really enjoyed being part of a gun crew as you fired hundreds of rounds, not like before where it was one missile a year; this felt like proper soldiering, it was what I joined to do. I wanted to be part of a gun crew, it was a man's world, firing shells, stinking of gun cordite, fast and furious, great stuff. Handling the guns and ammunition is not a job for the weak. You need to be strong and fit to survive. At all times you have to be alert; if not you will get injured. I also saw a finger being ripped off, the soldier was wearing a wedding ring, which was not allowed. He jumped off a lorry, his finger got caught on a bolt and the force of him jumping down and the ring catching on the bolt took it off.

One of the batteries went to Belize on a six-month tour; a soldier from the unit told me a story. Apparently his mate woke one morning, and when he turned his head to the side he was face to face with a big jungle snake. He said the snake had swallowed the man's arm and had stopped when he had reached the soldier's shoulder as the snake could not get the head in its mouth. It had got stuck and died. The soldier was said to have been asleep and his arm had fallen out of the camp bed. As it was hanging there the opportunist snake decided he had found a nice meal and swallowed his arm. Apparently he had jumped up and started to jump around, screaming. The soldiers with him jumped on him and cut the snake's body below the soldier's arm, at which stage the soldier fainted. The medics were called for him and the soldier was rushed off to hospital with the snake attached to his arm. Once the snake was removed they found lots of damage to the arm. I would never have believed this story if I hadn't bumped into a soldier years later who was actually there when it happened. People ask why he did not wake up when the snake started to swallow his arm. I can only put this down to the fact that sometimes on exercise you are so tired, you sleep through anything (once after a three day exercise with very little sleep a burglar broke into my house, knocked over a tin of paint and left the front and back door open. The house was very badly smashed up and the weird thing was I was on the settee the whole time, oblivious). I only woke up when I heard my wife screaming, 'There is someone in the house!' by which time he had fled. The story about the snake struck a raw nerve with me, I'm not a snake fan and it made me quite wary of leaving any of my body parts out of my bag.

Around the same time I woke to there being hundreds of police around the camp. One of the sergeants had lost the plot and had held the local post office up with a shotgun. Fortunately, he was caught within a few hours and carted off; apparently he just lost the plot. Also around this era there was a soldier who wanted to leave the Army but wasn't allowed due to his contract, so he decided to pretend he was mad and went around saluting everyone, one of my mates who knew him and said he did actually go mad and had to leave.

When it came to fitness tests I usually was in the top 25 per cent, I got a bit big for my boots and learnt the hard way that none of us is invincible, water is essential and if you're not sensible your body won't play! It does not matter how fit you are, your body will collapse if pushed too far when dehydrated. We had been on the rifle range all day on the hottest day of the year, and then we were put on parade and told that we were marching ten miles back to camp. This was an easy challenge; I'd done worse and had no problems. We had marched and run for about six miles when people started to collapse. We had thirty six pounds on our backs, rifle and helmets and I remember thinking, what's up with these people? My mate was struggling so I carried some of his equipment thinking I was superman. I remember starting to feel weak myself but because I was fit I just kept working through it. Little did I know what was going to happen next. I'd never felt like this before, I thought it must just be the heat. I suddenly fell out of the squad and ran over to the hedge by the side of the road and fell into it. The Battery Sergeant Major came up to me and picked me up and in my delirious state I told him to fuck off. This is the same man that I saw beating three soldiers on my first day in the battery. I told him I was not a waster and there was nothing wrong with me. I then tried to stand by myself and rejoin the squad but failed and collapsed back in to the bush. The next thing I knew I was waking up in hospital with five doctors and nurses standing over me. I did not know what was going on but my naked body looked like a prune, as if I'd been in the bath for hours.

'It is normally bigger than that!' I exclaimed.

They looked in dismay and ignored my statement. Apparently I had pushed myself through heat exhaustion, the body warning that you are getting too hot and lack fluids. The next stage, which is what I had, was heat stroke, from not drinking enough water throughout the day. Your body has a shut-off valve and once you hit a temperature it closes down. You have only a certain amount of time to get sorted out before your blood boils and you die. I was told I was chucked in a bath of cold water and pumped with fluids. It took a day before my memory came back and two months until I was fit again. On that march nine of us collapsed and ended in the hospital. It had been too hot and we hadn't put enough fluid in our bodies. As soon as I was fit they made me do the march again to prove to them it was a one off, and that I was not a waster. A lot of soldiers died on such marches until the Physical Training Corps tightened the procedure up and monitored the marches more efficiently. One of the fitness tests was an eight mile march with a pack weighing thirty five pounds that had to be completed within two hours. The problem was that units wanted to do it faster than other units, so sometimes you would complete it in one hour twenty. This pace was hard and people used to collapse all over the place. Tragically someone died of a heart attack, so the rules were changed. If the unit got back in under one hour fifty five, it was classed as a fail. This meant they had to go around the route in the desired pace of just under two hours.

In a unit you will have a range of varying fitness, from average to super fit, and those who just scrape the standard to pass the test. Most soldiers take pride in their fitness and work very hard at it. The basic fitness test in those days was a mile and half run that you first did as a squad in fifteen minutes, and then on your own. You had to do it in ten and half minutes. One lad could do it six minutes fifty-five seconds. Most people got in from eight minutes to nine thirty, with the unfitter getting in after ten minutes. If you failed the test you were put on remedial PT.

As a private soldier you sometimes had to do extra duties during the month, for example, guard duties, fatigue man (basically a litter picker and waiter if the officers held a function, as a soldier you learnt to just get on with it). The worse duty I had was to be waiter in the Officers' Mess for three months. I was told it was all part of my education, and that it would help me when I became a Sergeant. It was all crap, I was just in the wrong place at the wrong time and had to go and do it for a three month period. I thought it was disgusting that a man who joins to soldier has to wear a white shirt and bow tie and be a piss boy for young officers. My duties consisted of making tea, taking it to them, serving them at meal times and worst bit of it, they had to ring a bell and I would take their orders (humiliation at its best). In the Royal Air Force and the Navy you can join to be a steward, I thought they should have that system in the Army or better still, let the lazy sods do it themselves. Every day I begged my Sergeant Major to get me out of there, and every day he told me to fuck of and get on with it. On one occasion he said if I complained again he would keep me in there another three months, so I kept my mouth shut. It was so degrading in my eyes, I have never hated doing anything so much in my life. I joined to soldier not to be a piss boy to officers, I do not know how I got through the three months without being put in jail for having a crap attitude, I found it so embarrassing having to go to work with a white shirt and a bow tie. I think they employ civilians to do it now.

After my nightmare in the Officers' Mess I was sent to Cyprus for two months, attached to an Air Defence Battery to do infantry training. Although our primary role was to fire the guns, if you're in trouble and you needed artillery fire to get you out of it, you call for fire and normally get it where and when you need it quite promptly. It is something we are extremely good at. We also had to defend the gun position as the guns are seen as a priority target by the enemy; this meant we had to be trained in infantry skills too. I had a good time in Cyprus and was fortunate enough to meet a young lad who shot down an Argentinean air craft in the Falklands war. I was impressed with this: eighteen years old, at war, firing his first missile and achieving an excellent result. It was his first live missile and he shot the aircraft down on his first attempt. I think he was one of the only ones to do it due to some sort of technical problem they had with the equipment.

We had some young Paratroopers attached to us, unfortunately for them they had the attitude that if you weren't a Para then you were a wimp, this wasn't true as the Sergeant who was in charge of them found out. He decided to hit a young gunner around the face with his rifle butt. The young gunner turned around and gave the Sergeant probably the biggest kicking he had ever had, as well as to another Para who tried to help him, they kept a very low profile after that. The Para Sergeant could not report the gunner as he had struck the gunner with his rifle butt in the first place. Most units have some very high class personnel in it. The only difference between the army and the Marines and the Paras is that we don't have a filter system, i.e. selection. Consequently we have some muppets but I would say the top third of any unit could hold its own with the Marines and the Paras as far as fitness goes, and in my opinion we are better technically as we spend longer training on our equipment. On one of the exercises we had to do a beach landing. As the landing craft stopped, the officer in charge jumped in to the sea and shouted 'Follow me!' Unfortunately for him the landing craft had stopped too far from the beach so he went straight under. He surfaced with us all laughing at him. The Sergeant Major told the coxswain to go further in and we all jumped in at waist level, leaving the red faced officer bobbing up and down behind us in the deep water. After the exercise the officer was presented with a pair of kiddies' orange arm bands to aid his swimming skills.

Whilst in Cyprus I started work at five and finished at twelve so the rest of the day was spent on the beach getting a tan and being paid to do so. There were lots of snakes in Cyprus and because of the story about the man having his arm swallowed I was pretty scared of them. On one occasion we were all watching a film when someone threw a snake into the crowd, it was really funny watching about thirty men jump in to the air all screaming and trying to get away from the snake (which was already dead). I think I was probably one of the first out of the door. Someone also put a dead fish in someone's sleeping bag; it was hilarious watching the poor victim scream as he put his leg in to his sleeping bag, to be greeted by a solid wet slimy object. These kind of memories make me chuckle every time I reminisce.

After Cyprus we went to Edinburgh for a month and did the gun race at the military tattoo. This was great fun and the social life was great as well. After that I went to Denmark, attached to a Commando Battery. I played football with them and not one could catch me as I was so fast. The next week their BSM tried to recruit me to try for the Commandos but as before I declined, and yet again was called a crap hat and was told I was wasting a talent.

On my return to England I was told that the regiment was being posted to Germany to a place called Hohne, which was just outside Belsen concentration camp. It was the first concentration camp the British soldiers found at the end of World War Two. They had burnt all the huts down and paraded the locals to see all the bodies. It was the very railway sidings that the Jews used to arrive at where later we were to load all our equipment to go and fight in the Gulf. (I must admit I was extremely pissed off that I was going back to Germany, having had a great time in Colchester and thinking the social life of Germany did not compete with that of England.)

One of my last nights in Colchester was very eventful. There were four of us and someone had a great idea to go to a club where soldiers were forbidden, as local gypsies would go there with the express intent of fighting soldiers. We got in there and were separated and the next moment I heard a big ruckus going on. I saw my mates being beaten out of the club by about twenty gypsies. I was stuck at the other end and somehow had to get out to my mates without being battered myself. The only way was to get on my hands and knees and crawl along the floor of this packed night club. I eventually ended up being kicked about thirty times by the gypsies as my mates were out of the club by this stage. I was the only

one left, I did bite two calves and I think I broke someone's toes by hitting them hard, but yes we did all take a
battering. It was funny in the car going home, we knew
we'd been beaten but with four of us against twenty,
there was not much we could have done.

I always seemed to be taking train journeys from one
place to another. On one occasion a man came up to
me at the platform in London and after thirty minutes
of talking to me asked if I wanted to go back to his flat
around the corner for some fun. I replied,

'Wrong bloke mate, my ring piece is nice and tight and
it's staying that way, now fuck off!' He disappeared pretty
quickly. I thought he was just making polite conversation; it never crossed my mind that he had his eye on
my bottom. A con man also chatted to me and tried to
get money from me. He said if I didn't give him twenty
pounds he was going to stick a knife in me. It was one of
those situations where I had to think quickly so I stamped
on his foot and as he was hobbling about I legged it. I
did not feel safe until the train was moving and I was far
away. On another occasion everybody walking past kept
staring at me. I started to think that my hair was green or
something and could not figure out what was going on.
It was not until I looked behind me that I noticed that
Bobby Ewing from Dallas fame was behind me.

'I thought it was me, Bobby, that they were looking
at!' I said to him. He just smiled.

CHAPTER THREE

Capture

The regiment moved to Germany in 1985, I really didn't want to be back in Germany. After the war the British got the northern part of the country and the Americans gained the south. I can honestly say that the northern part of the country definitely would not have been my choice as I thought the south of the country was far more beautiful.

I heard a story of a soldier who hated it so much that he stole a British vehicle with floating capability and tried to use it to get across the channel back to England. It didn't work, of course, he was caught. A lot of soldiers loved Germany as you were paid more for being there and the drink, cigarettes and fuel were very cheap. For some reason I just preferred England, and still do. I have visited and worked in lots of foreign places but in my opinion the south coast of England is the most beautiful and if I'm honest I have found the English people on the whole are the best (apart from the odd twat like everywhere).

We were posted to a big garrison with two artillery regiments, an infantry regiment, a tank regiment and a Dutch unit. It is unbelievable how much fighting goes on between units. Every Monday morning on parade, men would be standing there with black eyes etc. from the fighting that went on between units in the bars in town.

People were defending their units and their honour against each other. On our very first day one of our lads walked into a bar to be met by a Welsh Guardsman's fist, with the words, 'Keep out of here, this is our bar!' On one occasion I was in a bar and one of our soldiers started on a Welsh Guardsman, there were nine of us and he was on his own, the Guardsman wanted no trouble and tried to leave, he was only a small man but as he got to the door he said,

'I am not having this!'

He battered five of our lads to get to the one who started on him and gave him a good beating. I was watching from a distance and thought it was good on him as our lad was in the wrong and deserved his battering. We did get CS gassed by the owner which wasn't pleasant. Another time, I felt sorry for a sergeant who was at the chip shop as two guardsmen started on him. Luckily he could look after himself and gave them a good kicking, although he was able to defend himself he ended up getting demoted to a Gunner and got six months' jail sentence. The good thing was that after his sentence he worked himself back up the ranks, was commissioned and is still serving.

We spent a long time training on our new equipment and seemed to be constantly on exercise; we would deploy for three weeks, then go back to camp, then back on exercise. We had left our FH-70 towed howitzer in England and were now equipped with the 155mm MI09 self-propelled howitzers. These were Americans guns that the British had bought from them. The regiment had to train hard on this new equipment to get up to speed and combat ready. One famous story that went round the Artillery was about an officer's dog. The officer in question always took his dog on exercise with him and this used to get on the gun crews' nerves. One day, the dog crapped on a gun crew's position, pissing them off so much that the gun crew loaded the dog in the gun barrel and blew him up whilst firing a shell.

There was a tradition on the end of exercise called the Mexican bum wank. At the end of the exercise some poor victim, normally the new boy, would be chased and once caught the fattest lad would take his pants down and stick his ring piece on the poor victim's nose. Considering he had been in the field for days without washing this was not the most pleasant thing to happen, I am glad to say this tradition got banned in the latter years.

During this time I was sent skiing for two weeks, which was fantastic. Regiments had their own ski huts and instructors and would send thirty men at a time to go and learn how to ski. I can honestly say that the two weeks that the Army sent me skiing was the most enjoyable thing that I have done so far in my life. It was funny watching us on the first day, all dressed the same in some old ski suits that were purchased second hand as a job lot, everyone falling over and bodies all over the place. The first three days it looked as though we were drunk as most of us were falling over, getting back up and then falling over again. The scenery and forest and mountains in the south of Germany are some of the most beautiful in the world, not like the dump we were posted in. At the end of the two weeks we were all good skiers and apart from our suits you would find it hard to pick us out from the locals, most of whom had skied from an extremely young age. In the Army you can easily get qualifications, such as ski instructor, glider pilot, football coach, canoeing instructor etc. The soldiers were instructed by soldiers who'd achieved the teaching certificates to do so. On this occasion an officer's wife had been sent on the trip with us because she had been caught having an affair back at camp. The Commanding Officer thought it would help save their relationship to have the other man posted away. I remember walking home one night to see my mate in the telephone box with his trousers down to his ankles and the officer's wife giving him oral sex. I don't think her relationship survived, but my mate had a smile on his face for days.

After all the training and exercises we began to have some more spare time and started to explore Germany more. The options we had were to stay in camp getting drunk in the battery bars, or to get out and explore the country. A lot of soldiers took the first option but I would say most took the latter. Lots of soldiers were married and lived on camp with their families, but if you were single then just hanging around the camp bars was a waste of your time. About three times a year we used to have strippers in our bar. The whole battery would parade there dressed in long johns, a t-shirt and a furry hat, which was the dress code for the function. On one occasion the Sergeants' Mess had strippers, but one of the wives reported it to the Sun newspaper and the functions where strippers were involved were stopped. One night whilst in the battery bar my mate said that he fancied going to the Harz mountains for the weekend to do some skiing and asked if anyone was interested. Another lad and I thought it was a great idea as we had just got back from skiing and had enjoyed it that much. I had no idea where we were going but at the time, especially after a few beers, it just sounded like a great idea. At half past four the following morning, after about two hours' sleep and still drunk from the night before, we set off to the mountains, which were about five hours away. I had no idea where we were going. We had basic clothing: jeans, coat, hat and gloves. We had no ski equipment and the plan was to hire it out from one of the local shops. The journey there was uneventful. I slept in the back of the car most of the way due to all the drink I'd had the night before. We arrived at the town at the bottom of the ski slopes and it looked the same as any ski resort. There is something magical about ski resorts. It was a beautiful place, the weather was fine and there were people everywhere, the slopes being particularly full. Excited and eager to get going, we parked the car and found the nearest equipment hire shop. We chose the equipment we wanted and then tried to pay for it but the lady said we could only have it if two of us left our identity cards as security. This was a big no-no, a soldier must keep his ID on his person at all times and never let anyone else have it (it is the size of a bank card with your details and picture on it). If you lost it you would go on orders and would be charged £50. One soldier lost his eleven times and was sent to a doctor as they thought he had some sort of mental illness. It was found that he was just one of those people who lost everything every day. The problem we had was that she would not let us have the equipment and if we didn't have the equipment we would have to go home. Eventually we gave her our cards and left the shop with our ski equipment. We could not know the problems this would cause us later that day and also into the months ahead. We bought our lift pass, which gave us about seven trips up and down the slope, and made our way to the top of the slope. Once at the top of the mountain we had a look at our options and decided to take the easy route first. We did this twice and then skied down a harder route on the other side of the mountain. The slope stopped half way down, and you were supposed to get a ski lift back to the top. However in seconds the weather changed. One moment the sun was shining, the next it was chucking it down with freezing cold rain. This was a major problem as we were not properly dressed for foul weather and within minutes we were freezing and starting to suffer with the cold. We had only been caught in the bad weather for a few minutes but we were wet and starting to shiver. Our cheeks were turning numb and I knew it only takes minutes for your body to start going downhill. We decided to get off the mountain but the problem was that we had to take the lift back up the side we were on, then ski to the bottom of the other side. We thought this would take too long and our condition would get worse, as the higher you go, the colder you get. We were already so cold that we decided it would take too long to do this, and we had noticed what looked like a toboggan slope on the other side of a small fence. It looked as if it went straight to the bottom of the mountain. Envisaging a nice smooth run, and desperately wanting the quickest route down to the warmth of the car heater, we set off. We made our way to the fence, which was only about seven foot in height. With the snow deep next to it, it wouldn't be too hard to climb. The fence looked no different than a perimeter fence around a school and we thought it was to stop people getting on to the toboggan track. One by one we climbed the fence (not easy in ski boots; it took us about five minutes). We then sorted ourselves out ready to ski again. At this stage the weather cleared but we were still wet and cold. My friend who had organised the trip went sprinting off in front of me and our mate. We started to make good progress and found ourselves going along at a good pace with my mate about two hundred metres in front of us. We thought we would end up at the bottom of the mountain really quickly, but little did we know what was waiting for us around the corner. My mate disappeared ahead of us, we entered the bend behind him, but as soon as we saw him again he had stopped and was standing there with his arms in the air with a soldier wearing a fur hat (he looked like the typical Russian soldier that you saw in the winter uniform in the films). This was the beginning of our nightmare. We stopped and looked at each other, slightly astounded.

'Oh shit!' my mate said, 'we must have skied over the border into East Germany!'

'What fucking border?' I replied, 'I never knew we were anywhere near the border!'

'Well I think we are,' he replied, quite calmly under the circumstances, although it was obvious we hadn't been too clever.

It was indeed the Inner German border; a fence dividing the West from the East. In fact the reason the British Army was in Germany in the first place was to stop the Russians invading Western Europe after the Second World War, when the country had been divided into Allied (British and American) or Russian hands. It was then that the border fences had been erected.

At this stage four more soldiers appeared, all shouting at our friend pointing their guns at him. When I look back it was a funny sight to see my mate standing there with his hands in the air and all these soldiers around him pointing their guns but at the time we did not see the funny side of it. They were about one hundred metres from us.

'Shall we make a run for it?' I asked my mate.

'Do you think we can make it over the fence in time without being shot?' he replied, a very logical answer showing that he was obviously thinking much more rationally than myself.

'Maybe,' I replied, 'but we can't leave our mate like this, plus these stupid boots will slow us down.'

It's the old Army thing that you never leave your mates. If twenty of you go somewhere, then twenty come back, even if you are carrying them in a body bag. I had seen the border on many occasions as border patrols were sometimes part of your duties. You'd patrol the border just to show the East Germans and Russians that you were around. I'd also been to Berlin and seen the border there. Berlin was in the Russian sector but was divided into West and East Berlin so you had a small amount of allied troops stationed there in the middle of East Germany. I think the troops there would have had a life expectancy of around three minutes if war had ever broken out. The borders I had seen were like World War Two fences with guards everywhere (the fence we had climbed looked nothing like it, with no warning signs and not a guard in sight). At this stage three of the other soldiers came running towards us shouting something which we took as 'Put your hands up and stand still!' so automatically we did just that. We were now in the same stance as my mate who was a hundred metres in front of us. I remember thinking, 'Oh shit, I am well and truly in the crap this time.' Two of them came behind us and started to point their guns in our back. This was done to make us walk to our other friend. I could see a tower in the distance which I immediately recognised as a guard tower, and it was the same as the ones that I had seen on previous border patrols. There was a bit of a mad commotion with the Guards shouting at us in German and taking our ski equipment off us. An officer came out of the tower and spoke in English he said to the first lad,

'Are you English?' he asked the first lad.'

'Yes,' he replied, 'we are British soldiers.'

His face lit up as though he had won the Lottery, he knew that capturing us was going to gain him brownie points.

So here we were, three soldiers, one twenty and two of us just nineteen, standing at gun point having accidentally crossed the East German border. We were the triggers of an international incident, and this within days would be at the desk of Margaret Thatcher. This had all happened within three hours of reaching the ski resort.

'Papers, your identification? the officer shouted.

My mate handed over his card but as the other two of us had handed ours over at the ski shop, we could not prove who we were. We were then searched to see if we had any weapons on us. The officer kept repeating,

'You are a soldier, who are these two?' It was as though they thought he was Special Forces and he was helping us to escape from East Germany. He kept going on,

'Why don't you have identification cards like your friend?' We tried to explain but I don't think he believed us. He looked at us as though we were lying to him. For about ten minutes we tried to explain why we had no identification. But then he shouted, 'Silence! Stand still, don't move!'

We stood there for about another five minutes whilst the officer went to the top of the control tower and I could see him talking on a radio to someone. We were then one by one escorted into the tower. It was on three levels, the bottom being the entrance and the store room, the second floor being the sleeping quarters for the soldiers and the top being the watch tower. We were put into the middle tower and told to sit on the bunk beds. I thought they wanted us to go in to the top level, I started to walk as if that was where I was going but was met by an angry officer who pushed me back down to the second level, screaming at me and pointing his pistol in my head. The hatches were then closed. All three of us were now in the room on the second level.

Suddenly, it went pitch black. There were three guards still in there with us. We were kept at gun point and told not to talk, so we just sat there in the darkness, for thirty minutes. Those thirty minutes were probably the longest of my life. It hit me, the shock of realising we'd messed up and were in big trouble. It is a traumatising shock to suddenly realise you have had your freedom taken away from you, and to be put in a strange, hostile environment where you cannot do anything but wait. Only an hour beforehand we had been peacefully skiing down a beautiful ski slope; now we were locked in a dark room with guns pointing at us. I think the worst was the not knowing what was going to happen. In your head you have visions of all the bad stories you've heard about these kind of situations, and once you've imagined what you think is the worst scenario, there's always an even more horrific one to conjure up in your head. It was pitch black so could not see my mates. I wanted to call the one who organized our little outing a twat for not knowing we were next to the border; if he'd said the mountain was near the border I wouldn't have climbed any fences. I thought the skiing resort we were going to was somewhere in Germany and it never crossed my mind that it could have been in a dangerous location next to East Germany. I was also dying for the toilet so this and my head doing somersaults about blame and my own stupidity was sending me a bit bonkers. I decided I was not going to ask to go to the toilet at this stage. Suddenly the hatch opened and there was light again, the guards started yelling at us, the officer who spoke English shouting,

'Get outside!'

This was all done with great urgency and they were defiantly stamping their authority and letting us know who the boss was. We were then met by another officer and about eight guards who had been sent to transport us to their headquarters. We were told to get onto a lorry which had four guards on it already. Again this was done with lots of shouting and in an aggressive manner. A guard sat opposite each one of us with a gun no further than two feet from our heads. There was one vehicle in front of us with an officer in it and one behind with more guards. They did not look like conscript soldiers but looked astute and very stern. After about a mile I noticed lots of soldiers skiing up and down the border (I guessed they had been called out to see if there were any more of us). We were told later when we got back that these were probably their Special Forces as they were all dressed in white ski uniforms. We then arrived at a fence which had a large iron gate which they had to open to get across the road. There was then another entrance which led to the same road we had been on before. Once through the two gates, the guards got out and started to rake the tyre marks out of the snow, this I imagined was so you could not tell if anyone had been through. The guard who had been performing this duty threw the rake back in to the truck, and it landed on my legs. I automatically bent down to lift the rake off my feet, the guards sprang into action and pointed their guns within two inches of my head and started screaming, I got the message pretty quickly and shot up and let go of the rake (the quickest I've ever moved). They thought I was going to use it as a weapon and were not afraid to use the guns. I think this was when we all became aware of the seriousness of our situation.

The scenery was spectacular, with mountains and forest and snow everywhere. It was a beautiful part of the world and would have been very enjoyable to look at had it not been for our unfortunate situation. I thought to myself that it would be good if they just took us to the border and let us go with no fuss, but I knew that was not going to happen. After what seemed like a life time but was probably only about forty-five minutes, we arrived at their headquarters in Magdeburg, East Germany. It was a large building with soldiers every-where outside, and the sound of guard dogs barking their heads off. When I think back to what happened it is always the sound of the guard dogs barking that sticks in my mind. We entered the building where some high-ranking officers told the guards where we were to go. As before, this was done with shouting and with great speed as though it was a well-rehearsed procedure. We had to go up some stairs as the room we were being sent to was on the top floor of the building. This was not easy in ski boots. All the time the guards were pointing their guns in our backs and shouting at us to get a move on. At the top of the building, we were put in a large, confer-ence type room with pictures of communist leaders on the wall and a large table in the middle. Each of us was placed in a corner of the room with three armed guards at the door. At this stage I was dying for the toilet due to the cold and the nerves, my bladder now the size of a child's space hopper. I asked if I could go but they did not speak English, so I held my groin and acted as though I was peeing. I must have looked like a total idiot. They smiled and took me to the toilet with their gun barrels no further than a foot from my head, unfortunately for me and them I then needed to go about every ten minutes for the next hour. I think this was due to the shock of what had just happened and the old habit of needing to pee whenever I was nervous ... I always seem to suffer from the peeing thing after one pint of lager as well. The guard just looked at me as though I was some sort of weirdo and was probably a bit suspicious by my constant need to use the loo. It was a little bit strange having to go to the toilet with two men in furry hats pointing their rifles at you. At least they let me go and I did not have to sit there and wee myself; a pool of smelly wee wouldn't have been nice.

After about one hour of staring at the wall, my eyes focusing on a black mark, it sank in that the situation we were in was pretty shit. My mate glanced over to me and was immediately shouted at to keeping looking to his front. They didn't want us to have eye contact with each other. An officer came along and called one of my mate's names out and told him to stand up and follow him. I think he was called first as he was the only one who had an ID card. I got a quick glimpse of him, he looked worried but tried to give me a nervous smile, all I wanted to do was call him a twat for getting us into this situation. Little did I know at this point that this was the start of the constant interrogation. About thirty minutes later the same procedure happened to my other mate and I was left on my own in the room with the guard at the entrance. I started to wonder why they didn't want to talk to me. The first lad returned after about one hour and I was then called for and was escorted to a room by two new guards. I had to walk down a steep set of stairs, the only problem was that I still had my ski boots on, which made manoeuvring quite difficult. Unfortunately I missed a step and fell to the bottom of the stairs, landing at the feet of some official looking officers. They stood there both shaking their heads, then I was picked up by the guards. They were looking at me as though I was some sort of muppet. I think the stupid nervous smile I had on my face did not help the situation and made them confused as to why I would find it funny. I was escorted into the room to find it was already occupied by three men sitting behind a desk, one of them in military uniform. It turned out that two of them were the main interrogator and his interpreter; the third man in a black leather jacket looked like a KGB man out of the films. (I was later told by our intelligence that he was probably the Russian representative and the other two were East Germans.) I was searched again and my wallet was taken out of the room to be checked. It was a small room with the three of them on one side of a table and me on the other. The main man started talking German which sounded like gobbledygook to me, then the interpreter began his job of deciphering what was being said. The problem was his English was very poor and he spoke slowly. It took ages for him to translate everything and became really annoying having to speak to him as though he was a two year old child. The first thing he said was that we do not know who you are and you need to speak and tell us everything from the moment you woke up today up until you were stopped by our soldiers. It is very important you talk to us as you are in a lot of trouble. I had to make the decision, do I stick to name, rank and number, or talk? This was not a war situation and I decided that if I stuck to just saying my name, rank and number, it would do me no good. I hoped to show them it was just an accident so I could get out of there. I also hoped my mates were doing the same. So I started telling him what we'd done that day. They kept interrupting what felt like every six or seven words to interpret what I was saying, going over and over my story until they seemed to be happy with what they had heard. During this time the man who I believe was the Russian representative did not say a word. After what seemed like hours they said I could rejoin my friends. I must admit I was in quite a bit of shock, but all they did was get our stories to see if they all matched up, so they could start to build a picture of what had happened and how we'd ended up where we were. Then the whole procedure replayed again and again, and we were forbidden to talk to each other. We managed to catch each others' eyes every so often, which I guess gave us some sort of security that we were not experiencing this horrendous experience on our own. Every time I got a glimpse of my mate who had organised it I just wanted to call him a twat but as we could not talk I had to wait until after the ordeal was over. I sat in the room again thinking about everything they had asked me and what my reply had been. I was satisfied that I had done the right thing, and just hoped my mates had done the same and that our stories were matching up. I was then called for a second time and I managed to get down the stairs in my boots without falling down them. I felt really chuffed that I had done so and smiled at the officers who had witnessed me full the first time.

As I entered the room I could see it was the same three that had questioned me before. This time, however, their line of questioning was totally different. Their first words were,

'Ok we have heard what all three of you have had to say, now it's time for us to ask you some questions.'

I was pleased to hear that my mates had not stuck to name, rank and number, and I was now sure that I had made the correct decision to talk. The first words they said to me were,

'The British do not know you are here … no-one knows where you are … and do you know what happens to spies in our country?'

At this stage my heart sank as I thought, 'This is it, I will go missing and no-one will ever know what happened to me!' I had crazy and scary visions of ending in a work camp in Siberia as some Mongolian sex slave. They thought I was James Bond, some secret agent or something. At this stage they had sent people out to check our car was parked where we had said it was, and someone had been to check out the ski hire shop and ask the women if three soldiers had hired equipment from her, giving our names to check on the ID cards. Their first question was about our unit.

'What job do you do?'

Now it was time to be clever. I had already told them what I had done that day to prove to them it was an acci-dent, but now we were going into things that I could not talk about.

'I'm just a private soldier' I replied, 'and do very little, I'm just a driver.'

That was a lie, I was part of an artillery self-propelled 155mm howitzer gun crew, but I didn't want them to know I was part of a team that could fire ninety six pound shells on to them. I thought they might get angry.

'Ok,' he replied, 'who is your Commanding Officer?'

'I don't know,' I said, quite desperately trying to sound like I had no fear as I didn't want them to know I was lying, 'I am just a private soldier who does not know what goes on. All I know is the man above me, and he is called Corporal, I don't know his last name.'

He then reminded me that the British did not know I was there and they didn't know who I was, and as far as they were concerned I was a spy. He then added again,

'Do you know what happens to spies in our country?'

That is when I thought, 'Oh shit, they really do think I am James Bond! This is getting worse and worse.' They said they were soldiers with a job to do, and if I was too then they understood the way that I was answering the questions, but if I did not help them to understand and find out who I was, I would not be going home, and no-one would ever find out where I was. This was the first mention of going home and gave me confidence as they had not said I was never going home. We were not at war in terms of a proper conflict, so I thought there was no point sticking to the name, rank and number protocol. If I had been captured on the battle field then I would have, but in this situation I am sure I would have gone missing in Siberia and would be there now as some big Russian's sex slave.

I imagine some high-ranking officers and soldiers who thought they were Rambo would reckon they would only tell their name, rank and number, all I can say is that there are times that you have to do what you think is right at the time, and not always do what the book says. The reason the Army is so good is that it is full of highly switched on senior non-commissioned officers who think on their feet and make the right decisions at the right time. A great example of this is in the Second World War when a commander was given a route with the sea on one side. Knowing that most of his unit would be taken out travelling down a narrow road with no way out on the seaward side, he got his Regiment on parade and told them their mission. He said that although it was standing orders that he should travel half way down the column, while the second in command leads the column, in this case he would travel in the front vehicle. He knew that this would give his men confidence as he was leading from the front and was certain to be killed. They did win the battle and he survived but it shows that thinking on your feet and not doing everything by the book can produce results.

One of the best lectures you get in the Army is the conduct after capture briefing. It is very useful and tells previous stories of capture and how to deal with the different situations. The worst fact is how many soldiers get raped, you are told that if you see your mate getting raped and he gets an erection then don't take the piss out of him because apparently it is the body's reaction in some men when something has been put up their backside. This happened to a high percentage of victims of rape so was proven to be not out of the norm (unfortunately in some cases they actually orgasm). You are also told to try and escape as soon as you can because the further down the line you go the harder the escape becomes. I am glad I never had this lecture before my experience; if I had I would have been really worried about being abused and getting a hard on in front of my mates, and even worse, being one of the ones who had an orgasm. The piss would have been taken out of me severely and no compassion or empathy would have been given to me by mates back home. I thought I will be helpful as I could, tell them things that made it look as though I was being really co-operative and helpful, but doing so by not telling them anything they didn't know already. I stuck to information that they would know from magazines, recruitment films, British military papers and regiment journals they could get their hands on. The Intelligence war was massive, all countries spying on one another and I wanted to make sure there was nothing I said that they did not know already. I then told them about my military career, what units I had been with and places I had been posted to. I missed out the bit about the Nuclear Missile Regiment which would have been a nightmare if they had found out about that. They would have had a field day with the information they could have got out of me. I was a qualified operator on the equipment and I think it would have made my experience a lot worse if they had found out. I mentioned that I had been to Germany before, but with the unit I was with now. I was scared that they could check my story out and find out I was lying. They then said they wanted to know all about my daily routine and if I did a lot of sports etc. I told them exactly and then was quite surprised when they asked me what we had to eat. I could not understand why they were so interested to find out how many meals we ate each day and what types of food we ate. They wanted to know all the details of all the little things that you did throughout the day, I think for at least an hour they asked about the type of meals we ate. After that what seemed like a boring and useless interrogation I was sent back up stairs. I went over everything they had said in my head and the words 'The British do not know you are here' and 'do you know what happens to spies in our country?' made me think surely they can't think I am really a spy. I was only there for about thirty minutes when I was called for again. The first thing they said to me was,

'What do you think of the communist system?'

I replied that I didn't know much about it, expecting them to give me a lecture of all the benefits of their system, but to my surprise they asked me if I would like to be a communist and work for them. I just smiled, and said,

'No, I'm happy with my own country and system.'

They then said, which obviously they would,

'So you don't like communist people? That is why you are in the Army, ready to fight against us?'

This wasn't good, I thought, they think I'm James Bond and I hate communism, so I said,

'I joined because I always wanted to go to Cyprus and be by the sea, I did not know I would be sent to Germany. I know nothing about communism apart from Russia is a great nation that helped us defeat Hitler!'

This seemed to keep them happy but I think they knew I was talking crap. They then produced the contents of my wallet and put an Edinburgh military tattoo gate pass in front of me, which had been left in there from half a year earlier when we had been part of a gun race team in their yearly display. I tried to explain it was nothing and it was just like an entry ticket, for some reason they were really interested in it, and kept asking questions about it for ages, as though it was some top secret document. It was so frustrating having to explain it so many times and have to listen to the interpreter trying to translate it at snail pace. When you have to speak like this you end up speaking slowly and like a two year old. The man who had been quiet in the background now joined in and kept on about the pass. I think they thought they would be able to copy it and gain entry to some military establishment. The man who I believe was the Russian representative kept on about the pass for at least an hour. I didn't mind this as I knew it was of no use to them. This was my third interrogation and I had no idea what time it was. I knew it was late, possibly around midnight and it had been a long, eventful day. At last my bladder had sorted itself out and I was not needing to wee every ten minutes. I was taken back to the room to find my mates still in the corners in silence. I really wanted to call my mate a twat and give him a big kick in his shin by this stage. After about another hour the guards then entered the room with a load of food: a selection of meats and cheese, and bread. It was put on the table and we were told to sit there and eat. The first thought that went through my mind was that it had been drugged, afterwards I found out my mates' minds had jumped to the same conclusion, we all ate very slowly for a few minutes but as we had not had anything to eat that day the hunger got the better of us and we tucked in to it. It was the first food we had had to eat since this morning at eight, when we'd been looking forward to our day of fun, exploring and skiing. It was a case of stay strong, keep your body fit and keep your morale high. It was extremely nice and we were more than ready for a Scooby-snack (in the interrogation brief they do tell you to eat food offered to you because you don't know when the next meal will be. Anything offered to you take).

Three camp beds were brought in and one was placed in each corner of the room and we were told to sleep, which we all did as we were absolutely exhausted from the constant worry of what was going on. Whilst we were asleep, still not knowing if this was going to get worse, our situation was starting to filter its way back to Britain. We found out later that once they had realised that what we had been telling them was the truth (all three stories were the same, that we entered their country by accident), they had contacted the British Government to tell them they had three of their soldiers and they were held prisoner because they had entered the country illegally. This was at the height of the Cold War; you can imagine the activity going on at the Ministry Of Defence and government offices. There was a spy swap going on in Berlin between the British and the Russians, an Israeli spy being swapped for a Russian one, so the two countries did not want our incident to mess the swap up (that was the reason it was kept quiet and not all over the newspapers and television). The first signals had been sent to our regiments informing them of our situation but of course we knew nothing of this and as far as we knew, we were well and truly in the crap and were heading for Siberia.

We were up early, it was one of those times you wake up and the first thought that enters your head is 'Oh shit, it wasn't a dream, this is really happening to me!' The two guards looked at me and pretended to have a wee, imitating what I did the day before when I got their attention when I needed to go to the toilet. They were taking the Mickey out of me, I think they were bored from guarding us for so long. But it shows that every soldier in every Army has a good sense of humour. The ongoing crap talk started again and one by one, we were taken back down to the next stage of the interrogation. In front of me they had a statement of everything that had happened to me, or their version of what had happened, they wrote everything out in their own words and didn't care that I obviously knew some of it was bull. I was told that everything was being taped and I was to sign the document. You are not supposed to sign any documents as it could be used against you, but I thought it is only a signature, what damage could they do with that? I did decide to sign it differently from normal. I read the statement but did not agree with it, they had put that we had seen the tower from the fence and had thought it was a ski hut and decided to ski to it. This was not true (they had said that so it did not look bad on their security). As the border was supposed to be secure we had exposed a major weakness, a blind spot where you could cross at will without being caught. As East Germans were always trying to escape to West Germany, this was serious. I am

73

sure a lot of questions were asked by their commanders why it was not until we had climbed the fence and been skiing for five minutes that one of their guards saw us. I refused to sign it, the tape was stopped and I was told that my friends had signed, and they were ready to move on to their next destination. I still very dominantly expressed I wasn't going to sign.

'Sorry, I am not going to sign it.'

'Ok,' they replied, 'your friends will leave you now and you have made things extremely difficult for yourself. We have told you that the British do not know you're here and as far as we are concerned you are a spy, we have bad punishments for spies. You have told us you don't want to be a communist, so things are looking very bad for you.'

I was not sure if this was a bluff, I had to think on my feet, I thought if I don't sign I'm going nowhere, if I do I might still not be going anywhere, but there's a chance I could get out of this mess ... I hoped my mates had signed it and it wasn't a bluff. Thinking about it, it seemed sensible not to upset these people any more. I did think that if they hadn't signed it and I did, I would look like an idiot and get the piss taken out of me for being a coward for the rest of my life. I weighed it up and took the gamble that the other two had signed their documents.

'Ok, I sign.' I thought if I got home I could explain the truth.

The tape recorder was put back on and I signed it. They asked me to say on tape that the treatment I had received from them had been fair, and that I was not ill-treated in any way. I agreed to this as the treatment had been good, we had been fed, kept warm and had been allowed to sleep and go to the toilet (about twenty times in the first few hours). I couldn't work out why they wanted that on tape, but it gave me hope that the British must know what had happened to us and my captors were covering their backs for when we talked to our people. I walked out of the room to find the other two lads there waiting in the corridor, it was great to see them and I was relieved my stubborn nature had succumbed for once and I had signed the document. I was told to stand with the others but we were still not allowed to talk to each other. Still no-one told us what was going to happen. We were escorted outside to where a small convoy of vehicles was standing, ready to take us to the next destination. I have a very vivid imagination and this was definitely a good scene out of a spy film. There were men dressed in leather coats and furry hats, they were great costumes and looking back it was quite funny, although at the time the last thing on my mind was finding what they were wearing entertaining. We were put in the back of a vehicle that looked like a Volkswagen camper van. There were four men in front of us, two guards, an officer and a driver. At the front and the back of us there was a car with four men all dressed in what seemed to be their daily soldier attire. This was the closest contact that we'd had with each other since we'd been captured. All three of us were crammed in the rear seat, we all looked at each other as to say how the fuck did we end up in this and more importantly, what was going to happen next.

The convoy set off and we started our journey to our unknown destination. It was strange, it was like travelling back in time in the sixties, we stopped at a railway crossing and the train that went passed was a massive steam train. The steam smoke was black and was aesthetically pleasing against the white snow. All the cars were the same style and looked very old. We had been travelling for a few hours when we saw a sign saying Berlin, we looked at each other and I think we all had the same thought that we were definitely going to Siberia. Someone asked where we were going and there was a quick sharp reply,

'Don't talk! Silence!'

When we entered Berlin I remember passing a T34 tank (it was one of the first to enter Berlin in the War, and it was there as a monument). I had been to West Berlin before on a rugby tour so remembered bits that I'd seen, which helped me get my bearings, and this gave me a slight sense of security. I think any familiar thing would have helped at this stage as everything was so alien and scary, my rugby lot had gone there on the Berliner train that was allowed to travel from West Germany to East Germany once a week. We went through areas where the windows had to be closed and there were guards everywhere. This was particularly distressing and I wished I'd not watched so much television and listened to so many stories of what happens to spies. From what I did see West Berlin was like any other western city; the east side of it looked completely different, as though it was fifty years behind in time. We arrived at two massive gates with Russian soldiers marching outside on duty. The gates were at least a foot in thickness. The soldiers were there in their funny uniforms and furry hats. They looked very alert, smart and as though they meant business. I did think at the time how impressive they all were, and looked forward to telling all my comrades, if I ever got back that was. The gates opened and we drove in to a small courtyard. My friends looked at me and I could tell we were all thinking the same, 'Oh shit, this is it.' I continued to predict that we were now being handed over to the Russians in a jail, and this was where their fun was really going to start. We sat there for five minutes with no-one moving, not even the escorts. Some people came out, they looked like KGB spies but this time they had a woman with them. We were told to get out of the car and the woman, sounding quite friendly, said,

'Follow me.'

We went into a room and were told to sit down. This was the first time that we didn't have the guards standing armed at the doorway; they waited outside. The lady asked if we would like a drink, I was ready for one, as my mouth felt like a sweaty sock. She told us that the British consulate would arrive in an hour and take us home. I can't explain how relieved I was to hear this. I finally got a chance to get out what I'd been thinking the whole time and called my mate a twat, we just laughed, but I don't think he realised how much I meant it. She said we could relax and talk to each other. It was the first time and a relief as the severity of our situation seemed to be coming to an end. She then went on to say,

'Can I ask you some questions?' She was pretending to have nothing to do with the interrogation side of things, I think she was trying to get information from us whilst we were relaxed and the guards weren't there. All the conversation in the room was probably being taped as well, she asked us numerous of times about the sort of food we had to eat at meal times. I think that all these questions on food and what we did all day was to find out how well trained and how well-looked after we were; whether we would stand and fight or walk away if we came under attack. The lady asked the same questions they'd asked us on the first interrogation, but she was doing it as if she was just passing the time in idle chit chat, but in my opinion it was just another way of them trying to get some useful information out of us, we all realised what was going on and did not say anything that could be of use to them.

After about a hour there was a knock at the door and two young looking, suited, official men entered. They told us they were the British Consulates and they were taking us back to a border crossing into West Germany. They explained what was going to happen and basically said that we were in a lot of trouble, and that there were a lot of people waiting for us back at the border. They asked if we had been treated ok and truthfully we could reply that we had. I must admit I was very pleased to see them and knew we were going home, despite the concern about how much crap we were in when we did get home.

CHAPTER FOUR

The Return

The consulate officials went off and spoke to the Russians. They filled in the paper work and then gave us the thumbs up that it was time to go, and finally we could get in the car.

When we got in the gates opened again and we drove in to East Berlin, the men started to chat more freely as we were out of ear shot from anyone who could have been listening. They told us that we had caused a massive international incident with the governments of East Germany, Russia and Britain, that everyone thought we did it on purpose, and that we were in a lot of trouble back home. He explained that we were being taken to another border crossing that was about three hours away, where the police and British intelligence would be waiting for us. He then asked us about our side of events so we once again told our story. He told us that we'd messed up, but one day we'd see the funny side of it. We were on a motorway somewhere in East Germany, there was snow and ice everywhere. Then, as if we hadn't been through enough, the driver lost control of the car and we skidded, the car spun and spun with us ending up in the fast lane with a big lorry coming towards us. It is said that when you are in a car crash it happens in slow motion, it is so true. I remember looking at this big lorry coming at us and it was happening in slow motion. One of the consulate officials started to scream and I was thinking to myself how my luck couldn't get any worse, first I skied across the border and now I was seconds away from being killed by a lorry. Somehow, the lorry managed to miss us and our driver started moving again. There was silence in the car as everyone was thinking of how close we had been to another disaster. We looked at each other and started laughing, although the two consulate men looked a lot more frightened than we did. The one who was obviously the boss was trying to reassure the driver, asking him if he was ok but for the next hour we took the piss out of the driver on his driving skills and how crap they were. This is yet again the difference between civilians and soldiers. To us it was just another event for us to have a giggle over and take the piss about. The relief at not dying and not having a gun pointed to our heads had finally hit home.

We arrived at the first check point expecting to drive through with no problem as we were with the British Consulate, and thought all the guards would have been briefed that three British soldiers were coming their way, as it was as official as you could get (the checkpoint was like any other international crossing, but with more armed soldiers). The guards hadn't been briefed and yes you guessed it, another stall to our return home. I sat there thinking, 'Crap, we're going to be sent back to Berlin!' They knew nothing about us and would not let us through, I was tired and from the look of the others, they were too. After about ten minutes and some phone calls we were let through. The same happened at the next checkpoint, and again at the final one, the last hurdle to getting back to West Germany. However after another ten minutes wait and more phone calls we were let through. As we crossed the border in to West Germany we were met by German and British military police cars. It looked like the American president motor convoy, there were flashing lights everywhere with at least ten cars with us. There were military police cars and the German civilian police as well. The shit was beginning to hit the fan, the scale of how much trouble we were in England hadn't dawned on the three of us.

Our car pulled alongside a building that was very close to the check point that we had just driven through and we were met by an Intelligence Corps Sergeant. The two Consulate men wished us luck and drove off back to Berlin. The Intelligence Corps Sergeant was a miserable twat who spoke to the three of us like crap and told us not to talk, and to sit in the corner of a room that he'd escorted us to whilst giving us yet more earache. I guessed this was probably the highlight of his career, having three soldiers to de-brief and question. In the Army some people don't do much soldiering and get a nice easy career. When you hear about ten thousand soldiers in a war zone such as Iraq, it was probably only three thousand who actually did the soldiering, while the others got off the plane, jumped on the coach, entered the camp then didn't leave the safety of it until they got on the coach to go home (in my opinion these are the people who you sometimes hear talking in the pub as though they had singly handed taken on the world, but in reality, they probably sat at a desk for their whole tour! You also get men who served for three years and hated every moment but when you hear them talk about their time in the Army they make out they were Rambo and loved every second of it. For me this muppet came under this last description.) Any soldier, unless you are a Royal Military Policeman (or a total tit), would have realised that three of his comrades had been through some bad

81

stuff and would at least talk to them with respect (even if they had a job to do.) The soldiers we met afterwards were considerate and empathic; some laughed and had a joke about it, which was really important to us at this stage as we felt like we'd been through the mill. The constant questioning started again; one by one we were to be interrogated by an Intelligence soldier. We were told not to speak unless told to and were not offered a drink or any food (in those days I smoked and he would not let me have one, which really pissed me off). The way he spoke to me made me quite angry, I thought well I'm in the crap, what difference it would make if I knock him out, I was seconds away from doing it when there was a knock on the door it was our Regiment's Orderly Officer. He came in and asked if we all right, I said yes, apart from this twat who's going to get knocked out. I told him how the Intelligence Corps Sergeant was treating us and after a quick word his attitude towards us was slightly better. (Looking back now I can see how outspoken I was. This I guess helped me with promotion but sometimes could be a shortcoming as I would get myself into trouble.) The Orderly Officer said that we were in a lot of trouble and would be going to jail, and that he would pick the three of us up in the morning and take us back to the Regiment. He gave me a cigarette that I smoked straight away, blowing the smoke in the Intelligence Sergeant's face in a small personal victory, revenge, a trait I have carried all my life. I was actually being obnoxious deliberately as the Intelligence Sergeant truly believed we had done it on purpose, he had come to the conclusion that we thought it would be fun to go over the border. The Government had classed us as three jokers and wanted us punished for it.

Once they had listened to what we had to say and realised it was an innocent accident, they started to lighten up a bit. We were kept there throughout the night, with no food, and having to sleep on the floor of a waiting room until our Orderly Officer would come and pick us up in the morning. The Intelligence Sergeant told us that we should have only told them our rank, name and number, that we should have not signed any documents and should have not talked whilst the tape was recording. We replied that if we had done this we would still be there; this being a strange situation with us not actually at war. He told us that his mission had been to find out what actually had happened and report the story to the top brass who were waiting eagerly to find out, so that they in turn could brief the government and the prime minister. He told us that he was pleased it had only been an accident; he would tell everyone that it had been a mistake. The problem was that a lot of high ranking officers wanted blood. He was proving not to be such a complete tit as I had first thought. When the Orderly Officer finally arrived and picked us up; he started laughing and said that we looked a right state, you can imagine what we looked like as we were still in our ski suits and ski boots and hadn't washed for days. He told us that he'd been told to drop us off at our Battery Sergeant Major's Office, he didn't know what was going to happen to us but he thought we could be going to jail. We arrived at our camp after a long, quiet journey, the three of us busily thinking of what had happened to us over the last few days and what laid in store for us now. We thought we'd be going straight on Commanding Officer's orders and then to Colchester for a nice long jail sentence.

We were marched into the Battery Sergeant Major's office who listened to what we had to say, simply asked if we were ok and then put us in front of the new Battery Commander (it was his first day of appointment), and we told him our story.

'This is not a good start to our relationship,' he replied, and told us that he was now going to brief the Commanding Officer. We were then warned for office, this is where you are told that you will be going in front of the Commanding Officer on orders to be sentenced.

The Battery was put on parade and was briefed on our story; this was done to stop all the false rumours that could have flown around, naturally everyone found it hilarious and constantly took the piss out of us. One soldier took the Battery flag down and replaced it with a Russian one, which had the regiment in stitches. That was until the Battery Sergeant Major saw it and went on one: it was taken down as quickly as it was put up.

We had to wait three months until we were put in front of the Commanding Officer, so in the meantime we cracked on with our normal work. On regular occasions we had to go for more debriefs with the Intelligence Corps who had an interest in how we'd been treated and interrogated, and wanted to know how our captors went about finding information from us. They also wanted to know what sort of questions we'd been asked. These meetings went on for a long time, they wanted to know if we'd been contacted by the Russians, as they thought we'd be approached to join them. We even had our bank balances checked to make sure we were not doing a little deal and making some money to supply them with information. Eventually we got to travel back to the ski shop to return our ski equipment and get our ID cards back, in those days we didn't have a lot of money and we were stung for the extra days' hire. The lady in the shop told us that the day after we'd hired the gear some strangers had come in to the shop enquiring if we had hired equipment from her (these were obviously the Russians confirming our stories). It was quite nerve racking being so close to the border again. I really did not want to be anywhere near it and was glad to get away as soon as we had returned the equipment.

We had to wait three months to see if we were to end up being incarcerated, everyone kept saying 'You are well and truly in the shit!' and 'You definitely will go to jail.' The rumours were that we'd get six months in Colchester jail. I had a lot of sleepless nights worrying that due to a stupid accident I was probably going to jail and then would be kicked out of the Army. This wasn't nice at all as I loved the Army, it was my life and all I'd ever wanted to do was be a soldier serving his country. It was amazing how many people come up to us repeating the rumours they had heard. People were saying they heard the BSM say that we going to jail, or 'I was in RHQ and I overheard the officers talking about you and they said you would be going to jail!' Getting incarcerated for me would have been horrific, I was blessed to have had a good upbringing with my father being an officer in the Air Force, it would have brought a lot of shame and I would have felt like I'd have let them down badly. Another rumour was that someone heard the BSM talking and he thought we were getting two years. It felt like the longest three months of my life. I felt sick when the big day finally came and it was time to go on orders and find out our sentence.

The whole format was horrible. The day before, you have uniform inspections with your Battery Sergeant Major, as when you are on orders you have to wear your parade uniform and best boots (which incidentally have to shine like glass). On the day itself you are put in a line outside the Regimental Sergeant Major's office. He inspects you, briefs you, shouts at you, and then shouts at you some more, then briefs you again – and then again, making it clear that if you mess up the drill entering the Commanding Officer's Offices the punishment would not be pleasant. The Provost Sergeant is there, waiting with members of the guard to march anyone who has been sentenced to jail, straight to jail at double time. There were about nine of us on orders that day, all for different crimes. The Provost Sergeant told us that the ones who go in last are the ones who normally go to jail, and guess what? You got it, we were the last ones to go in. No-one could imagine the apprehension and nerves that were going through my body, physically, from head to toe I felt like I've never felt before.

We watched the others march in and out, in some cases it went smoothly, some not so well, people were being yelled at and were having to march back and forth until they managed to march into the office sufficiently well to meet the RSM's standard. It came to our turn. The Provost Sergeant was standing there, two Guards were smiling at us; it was as though he was getting excited at the thought of having some new inmates to play with. The RSM came up to us and whispered,

'You know what is expected of you, if you mess the drill up and do not enter the Commanding Officer's Offices perfectly, we will be drilling you up and down the drill square for an hour just like some of the poor victims you've seen.'

Then came the order, 'Quick – march!' and we were drilled in at quick time. As soon as we entered the Office we were met by a wall of faces. The Commanding Officer was sitting at his desk, the adjutant beside him and our Battery Commander standing there to give us a character witness. We halted, and then right turned to face the Commanding Officer. Our drill had been good enough and we were left there to accept our punishment. The procedure consists of the following: the Commanding Officer reads out your name, rank number and you confirm who you are. He then reads out what you are charged with, in our case it was illegally entering a foreign country which actually was an offence in the Army law book.

He asked if we were guilty or not guilty, and we all pleaded guilty. The Battery Commander then read out a character reference, which said we were all good lads. The Commanding Officer then said,

'I award you a fine of one hundred pounds,' and went on to ask if we would accept his award or go for a court martial (this option is there if you feel you have been hard done by, in which case you would go in front of a General. The problem with this is that if you are found guilty the punishment is often worse). We were so relieved that we were not going to jail that we all said yes. We should have been marched out of his office but he ended proceedings and said he wanted a quick word. He told us the powers that be wanted the three of us put in jail for six months and then kicked out of the Army. But he had thought our case was a complete accident and a silly mistake. (This is a good example of an officer looking after his men and not being scared to fight their cause when he feels that they should be looked after.) He was more concerned and angry about the fact we had given our ID cards at the ski shop than us crossing the border. He could live with the accident of the border but giving up the Identity Card, he said, was very poor soldiering. He said that it was good that his soldiers got out at weekends and explored Germany (I guessed he was chuffed that not all of his soldiers got pissed at the weekend in the bars in camp). He did add,

'Next time, don't go anywhere near the border!'

We had been fined one hundred pounds for a tour of East Germany and Berlin which I thought was great value. It would have cost loads more if I had booked it through Thomas Cooke. The worst thing that came out of it for me was that I could not be promoted for a year, and was not supposed to use the radio due to the Russians picking up my voice and knowing where my unit was operating.

After our little escapade, all the units in Germany published routine orders about not going near borders, and soldiers were educated on the whereabouts of the border in the Harz Mountains. Apparently this should have been common practice before our incident. Unfortunately it took what happened to us to educate the other soldiers about what to avoid.

A boxer in training: the trophy at my feet is the 'Best Boxer' award.

The missile where my glove got caught in the fin before firing.

Myself and my brother.

Me, dad and my brother at Buckingham Palace.

The Berlin Wall.

The Checkpoint Charlie border crossing in Berlin.

On exercise in Germany.

My brother (right) and I during the Gulf War.

My gun, during the Gulf War, doing maintenance.

Me in the turret of my gun, manning a 50 cal. machine gun. The picture shows the sky, black from the burning oil fields, and a crew member's Union Jack shorts flying on the radio antenna.

Top: Relaxing in a trench during the Gulf War.
Centre: The gun in the desert, under its camouflage net.
Above: Our gun in the rocks where the news report was filmed.

GULF WAR
GUN PROGRAMME

Use both sides   Date 2⦶/02/91   Battery 38 ⫘   Gun B   Army Form W3981 (1977) (pads of 50)

INTERPOLATION		1	2	3	4	5	6	7	8	9	10	11	12
Bearing	Elevation	Target No. or Line No. or Serial	Time (mins) From	To	Shell and Fuze	Charge	Prop Nature	Fuze Setting	Bearing	Elevation	No of rounds	Interval in seconds	Remarks
	⫘	ONE			HE L116	8		60·8	104	686	5	control A/A	✓
													ALL
	⫘	TWO			ALL	ALL	⫘	62·8	233	712	ALL		RDS
													AMC
	⫘	THREE			SERIALS	SERIALS		57·5	256	639	SERIALS		

Printed in the UK for HMSO D6416830 6/95 PRP 5892Q

The gun programme depicting the raid where our guns were first fired in anger.

Prime Minister John Major thanking my gun crew for the work we had done in the Gulf War. I am standing on the far right.

Running the London Marathon.

My two poorly children: the reason I left the army.

CHAPTER FIVE

Promotion*

After the border incident I cracked on with my soldiering. The good thing about the Army is that once you have been punished for your crime, it is forgotten about. This allows you to carry on with life as it was before you dropped yourself in it. My soldiering now consisted of exercises, courses and sports competitions. Each regiment is normally good at a certain sport and in our case it was the tug of war; we were the Army champions. I tried this sport once but could not move my arms for hours afterwards due to the pain so I gave that up as a bad idea. The lads in the team would train constantly for the sport, they did this for six months and trained very hard. They used to walk around every day carrying sand bags to build their strength up. It was done like this because it looked good for the Commanding Officer's Report if his regiment was the top at something. Of course sport is good for building team spirit and keeping you fit, there is a lot of competition between each regiment and every soldier is encouraged to participate in something.

---

* In this chapter and elsewhere in the book, please note that all facts and systems are described as I personally remember them, and that different units may have had different procedures. Furthermore, my experiences may well differ from the those of the soldier of today.

When I was in the missile regiment they were sports mad. As they only fired one missile a year they had a lot of time on their hands, so could concentrate on the sporting side of life. If you were in the boxing team and the athletics team you could find yourself in a tracksuit eleven months of the year, although you did have to be excellent at your chosen sport to get in the team. Whilst I was in the missile regiment, our four by four hundred metre relay team had the third fastest recorded time in Britain for that year. I was a good rugby player and played for the regiment, this helped to get me a good profile and to get noticed by those above me.

When one of the lads broke his neck in a tackle, I was put off competing. He ended up in a wheel chair and not walking for the foreseeable future, probably never again for the rest of his life. I stopped playing rugby at the age of twenty three as fear of ending up the same way got the better of me. I did come out of retirement at the age of thirty, but within the first five minutes was carried off with a broken nose, damaged neck and a snapped hamstring muscle. That was definitely the end of my rugby career. I did win the one hundred and ten metre hurdles on athletics day, however; my mate broke his leg in the warm up, and so I got tasked to replace him (I was part of the sprint relay team). I stood on the start line in front of several hurdles that I had never jumped before, they looked a little too high for me as I only have little legs but I was going to give it my best shot out of fear of embarrassment. I ran as fast as I could with no knowledge of technique or style to get me over the hurdles. I could hear every one laughing on the side line but somehow I managed to win (the others couldn't have trained that hard). After that the man who was running in the four hundred metres dropped out, I heard my name being called out to take his place so I hid in the toilets until the race was over. A Sergeant Major had to do it instead and came last. I couldn't believe it when I returned and he gave me a bollocking. The thought of sprinting around the four hundred metres made my heart sink, so delaying my return from the loo was worth taking a bollocking for. I was fast over three hundred but the last hundred was a killer. I was called again for the long jump, I came last in that one, what did they expect with my miniature legs? Then after all that, I had to box again. I didn't want to, and ended up losing my fight. My opponent was a scarecrow. He had what looked like extensions on his arms, they were really long and I could not get near him, plus his boxing skills were excellent and put mine to shame. On the same night a lad was punched in the head, he collapsed and ended up with severe brain damage. This was really sad as he would spend the rest of his life like this, in those days you didn't wear head guards for protection as that was something that came in later on. We didn't have any one to represent us in the heavyweight category so one of the lads put weights in his pants to make the weight, even though he knew he was going to get destroyed in the ring. He did it because he got a point for the team, and yes he did get destroyed but here was another example of pulling out all the stops to win (if he hadn't done it the Sergeant in charge of the team would have boxed him anyway for not gaining them the extra point).

If you get noticed by doing sports, work hard, pass your courses and most of all do not get in to trouble, you will earn your first stripe.

After three years' man service I was promoted to Lance Bombardier. This was not a fast promotion, it was about the average experience and time under the belt one usually had, and this wasn't bad for me considering eleven months was wasted in the Missile Regiment. I don't think people realise how hard it is to earn your stripes and the training and qualifications you need to get promoted, and also I don't think people realise the responsibility that goes with each promotion. The promotion ladder is as follows:

Lance Bombardier or Lance Corporal
Bombardier or Corporal
Sergeant
Staff Sergeant
Warrant Officer Class Two
Warrant Officer Class One

I was in an environment of intense competition; there was a tremendous amount of highly motivated and ambitious young men fighting to earn the next promotion, and promotion means money. Here I will list the procedure that a soldier has to go through, to make it to Warrant Officer Class One.

In a fighting sub unit that consists of around one hundred and twenty men you will have about twenty two Lance Corporal slots, twelve Corporal slots, ten Sergeants, one Staff Sergeant and one Warrant Officer Class Two. There are normally four sub units in a Regiment and one Warrant Officer Class One slot (RSM for the regiment).

To earn promotion to Lance Bombardier you had to pass at least two courses, basic level and an advanced course in your trade. They weren't easy and required you to be very technically trained at your chosen trade; mine was Gunnery. To make a ninety six pound high explosive shell land in the right place it should do over a distance of eighteen miles, it takes an immense amount of very technical expertise. Completion of the entire training took about eighteen weeks of technical courses and you would spend approximately three years actually experiencing your trade, hands-on, with the equipment. At the start of the hands-on you would be given the piss boy jobs, such as running around the camouflage net holding the bag of pegs that are used to peg it in, and passing the shells to the loaders, then having proven yourself you would move up to a more senior job, such as loader, and then the man who operates the gun sights, or the driver. I always used to remind myself that whatever you do, even if it's picking up litter, if you do it well you will get noticed, and eventually one day get your recognition. As well as this work experience you would do a month's leadership course, this was designed to test and teach your leadership skills and basic soldiering knowledge. This particular time in my army career was hard, and I basically got beasted for a month. I had little sleep and got tested on my leadership and military skills thoroughly. As you can imagine there were thirty motivated, young, ambitious fit men all competing to do well. It was difficult and I had very high expectations of myself, which later on in life served me well (some of the men just wanted more money and some weren't as ambitious as others). The day started about five in the morning with a vigorous gym session, run or route march, followed by room and kit inspections (everything has to shine and look neat). The day consists of more lessons and personal training, you get about five minutes to eat and are rushed from activity to activity. At night I had more lessons and had to give lectures on various subjects, I finished about eight then I had to prepare my kit for the next day, you were lucky to get four hours of sleep a night. One night we moved my mate, fast asleep in his bed, on to the parade square, where he awoke in the morning with the RSM waking him up and shouting at him for being asleep in his bed on his precious drill square. We had a good laugh over that one. Unfortunately for my mate he did get drilled up and down the parade square by the RSM for thirty minutes. Another favourite trick of the training team was to give you changing parades, where you had two minutes to be dressed in whatever uniform they had stated. This went on for about ten different parades until the whole contents of your uniform was in a big heap by your bed as you just chucked it on the floor getting in to the next change of uniform. You can imagine what the rooms looked like with thirty men's uniforms every-where. At the end of the course you had a final exercise where you were beasted for about five days and had an average of three hours' sleep. On this exercise I had to do a river crossing. The river was fast flowing, I had forty pounds of weight on my back, plus a rifle and the anti tank weapon; all in all I had about sixty pounds to wade across with. I fell and went under, I just couldn't get my head above water, the weight was pulling me down. I spent about a minute on the river bed until I was lifted out by the training staff. I was quite scared, but perturbed at the fact the weight had got the better of me. They say drowning is supposed to be pleasant but I can assure you it is not. This was all done to see if you could handle the pressure when you're tired, wet, cold and hungry. You are tested on your map reading skills – yes, map reading is easy when you are on a road with road signs, but at night in the woods in pitch black when you are leading a section of eight men (and if you get lost you know they are going to think you're a twat as this means more miles to walk and less sleep) – it is not easy. You lose a lot of men through injury and just not wanting to face the challenges and the unknown that lay ahead of a soldier. I found that these courses suited the men who shouted a lot and made everyone aware he was there, the ones that liked to be centre of attention and stand out in a crowd. I was not like this and didn't want the attention as I was a quiet boy and at that stage lacked self-esteem and confidence. I did well enough to pass, though. My report said, 'This man is too quiet and we did not even know he was here until he collected his certificate at the end!' My friend's report was quite funny though, apparently 'he would look scruffy naked'. This friend was unfortunately killed whilst on exercise in Canada on a training exercise with another soldier from the battery. They were asleep in a tent when a vehicle ran over the two of them, crushing them to death. The whole battery went to their funerals and every soldier there wept liked babies for their lost comrades. Soldiers face death and will put it to one side and carry on with their jobs, but when the time comes to mourn will cry and let their feelings out. Being in an environment where you are trained to kill, tragedy is inevitable and this can be quite saddening and put a dampener on the soldier's spirits. During my career a lot of soldiers were killed and died in tragic accidents. I have mentioned some already and will mention more in the book, but at this stage would just like to add the following in respect to all those that served with me who lost their lives.

REST IN PEACE

The bells, they tolled as you entered through
  the gates,
The guard of honour was formed by your fallen
  mates.
The guns of war are silent now; you will not
  hear them any more,
You are sleeping with the angels, now and for
  ever more.

I always thought there was a time to shout and scream and when you did it was because you meant it. Shouting I believed had its place and a purpose and should be used sparingly. If there was over-use, the message you were trying to get across wouldn't work, in my opinion it's done to set a particular atmosphere and to get someone motivated; using it to impress or get attention etc. was a load of rubbish and not good leadership, and not a good way of getting people to raise their standards or do what they wanted. To me, surely a good leader is one who can get things done without the ranting.

I remember the exercise element of the course most, where we had to escape and evade, which was great fun. We were chased over three days by a hunter force of forty men until we were caught, then stripped of everything apart from some old clothes. I was searched to make sure I had no food or money and then was sent into the countryside. We were given just a map, it was in the middle of winter so you did get extremely cold and agonisingly hungry. The exercise is planned so that you get caught in the end. You have to go to check points and be met by a friendly agent, who tells you where to go to next the agent. They sometimes gave you one biscuit between three of you, normally at the last checkpoint if you made it that far before you were captured. It is done in a realistic way, which means it's meant to try you and not be easy, this is to prepare you for the real thing, and you normally take a few kicks during the initial capture. They put sandbags over our heads and stripped us naked and we were told to lie in the snow for an hour before our questioning. Out of twenty five of us, there were only seven who managed not to give in, they eventually said the exercise was over. Apparently if they had left us lying there any longer we would have gone down with hypothermia. It's shocking the extremes we went to, to qualify in these tests. A few years later I was the hunter force against the TA SAS, I had my six man team and own helicopter for three days, it was great fun, especially when we caught one of them. The SAS soldier tried to put up a fight, he got a few kicks and ended up tied up naked against a tree with a note attached to him, abusing him and his unit for being caught so easily (I must admit during the exercise we did not see any of the others, and it was only one of them who got caught so they were good at what they did).

I also had to kill a chicken which I found most horrifying, it's strange, I wouldn't think twice about putting a bullet through an enemy but killing a chicken I found quite emotional. This was the case with a lot of my fellow colleagues. At the start of the exercise a rabbit was given to me to be looked after, and at the end I was made to kill it for food. A lot of soldiers found this quite unbearable, of course if they were in a survival situation they would do it, so they had to be prepared for anything they may encounter at war (when they knew what they would be eating in the cookhouse the next day, they didn't want to eat their little buddy).

At the end of the course you get recommended for promotion straight away, after six months, twelve months, or not at all. I remember the first time I walked with my stripe on my arm, I thought I had made it to the top and never dreamt that I would make it any further up the promotion ladder. I was full of pride and felt as though all the hard work had been worthwhile. I was like a woman who looks at herself in the mirror all day every day, and my stripe was my goal achieved. The first stripe's quite easy to earn and, they say, the easiest to lose. The Troop Commander puts you forward and if there was a vacancy and you had the relevant qualifications passed, you normally got it. The Commanding Officer has the power to promote you at regimental level, this promotion gives you an added responsibility, and you are normally second in command of a small detachment with a corporal in charge of you. One of the good systems in the Army is that the rank below you can normally step in and do your job (if for some reason you are taken out). When you think about it, it is really important that there is someone who can step in to someone's shoes especially when units can have extremely high casualty rates. If I was killed then the senior gunner would take my place, and if my bombardier was killed I would take his place. This is why you have to be well trained and know what job the rank above you does, and be able to carry it out. Often on exercise you used to have second eleven training, where you would do the job of the rank above you. The Army is a business where people are killed, but has to keep on performing with the people that are still alive. This promotion made me the second in command of a gun crew with about five gunners under me and a full bombardier or sergeant in charge of us. Some people find it difficult to adjust to the promotion as you have to distance yourself and be authoritative. Some people get jealous, angry and frustrated with the change and you can lose friends. I had to reprimand them when they were under my command, and this is where I learnt how to deal with promotion. My trade as a Junior Non-Commissioned Officer was not going to be all glory and I soon realised that not everyone would like me. Not everyone is Non-Commission Officer material (these are normally the barrack room loafers who have no idea and would crumble if they had to lead men under pressure), they often can talk the talk, but can't walk the walk. These pains can often be found in the bar slating those in charge of them. You do get good soldiers who should be promoted, but seem to get into trouble. This slows down their progression and sometimes stops them from achieving their full potential, which is a shame as it means they lose out, not due to incompetency but because of their own doing. The soldiers who never really achieve and demonstrate their competencies one hundred per cent always regret their ignorance as they grow out of their childish pranks and behaviour. Some soldiers are let down by their drinking habits, for example, if they didn't know when to stop. If I knew then what I do now I would educate them, kindly and subtly, of their shortfall, just in order to help them. A lot of soldiers did drink every night and would always be found in the bar, but I would say this was a low percentage and most have normal drinking habits. I think one or two were alcoholics but it probably works out to be the same percentage as people in Civvie Street. I used to think alcoholics were just piss heads who just wanted to get pissed but I learnt it is an illness that you are born with. In America a doctor needed body parts for experiments and was told to go where all the alcoholics hang out by the docks as she would always find a body there in the morning. This she did. At a dinner three months later, she told some doctors it was so strange that all the drunks had cocaine in them. They replied, 'Don't be stupid, they can't afford that!' Doing tests they found they all had the same chemical in their brain. This chemical was looked at as a substitute to morphine but it was found that it was ten times more addictive than morphine, so could not be used. They found that when someone without the genetic defect drinks alcohol the body clears it out one hundred per cent; those with the defect cannot clear it all, and a chemical from the alcohol flows around the body and then sits on their brain. It does this for years and is of no harm until one day it releases from the brain and is released from the body. If you drink the addictive nature of the chemical makes you want more, hence you become an alcoholic; if you don't drink it is not a problem. It is not that they are twats, they have this genetic defect meaning that you can drink for years not knowing you have got it until it is released from your brain and that's it you are now the alcoholic. One lad was good but when he was drunk he did stupid things, such as bite the head off someone's pet hamster. He tried drowning people when they were relaxing swimming, and gave a soldier from another regiment a blow job for a crate of beer (he had no money).

The next promotion is to Corporal or in my case, Bombardier. To get promoted to Bombardier is slightly harder, again firstly you must have the relevant quali-fications and be very technically qualified and have passed your trade courses at Detachment Commander level. Also I had to complete another leadership course, the Detachment Commander level being the top course at your trade. After you have finished that you are technically as far as you can go with that particular equipment. You would have done about twenty four weeks of technical courses to get to this level and have about five years' experience on the equipment, as well as eight weeks of leadership courses. With this promotion comes the big boy responsibility, you are normally in command of a detachment and the buck stops with you if the detachment makes a mistake. This is normally your best soldiering rank, with you either in charge of an infantry section or a gun detachment, it is hands-on, and doing what I did best, soldiering! When you hear of soldiers on operations it is mainly at this level, they do the main soldiering jobs and are the feet on the ground. This is why when you hear of soldiers being killed, they are normally very young as they are the ones doing the fighting. You are very well trained but still young. You will have had approximately six years learning your trade and are now the subject expert. The real soldiering comes in the first ten years; the higher up you go, the more desk jobs you do and not so much hands-on work. You are not as technically skilled later as you were when you were the Detachment Commander, as in your later years you normally only spend two years in a role. In the later stages of your career, the Army is after your management and soldiering skills, and essentially your years of experience. There is a long way to the desk in the Army because you are dealing with people's lives; it's not just a normal day to day job as a mess up can mean the difference between life and death; a mess up could mean you end up spending time in prison.

I remember when I passed my technical course, I was told, 'Remember, now you have that tick in the box, the Army are covered. If you make a mistake whilst live firing, they will say you are qualified and you have been trained up to standard.' They explained I could find myself in charge of a multi-million pound piece of equipment and responsible for firing a ninety pound shell, within one hundred metres of our own troops. At the age of twenty three, this was a daunting prospect, one little mistake, easily made (especially when you have not slept for days and you have information coming to you quickly), would cause catastrophe. The information I was given I had to take on board and then pass on. I had to carry out technical drills on equipment and one slight mistake could cause death to my own troops. This rank I think is probably the best rank for soldiering as you have your own detachment and on the whole you are left alone to manage it as you feel fit. I was responsible for them and my decisions in war could make all the difference. In peace time you make sure they are trained and basically become their mother, father and brother, there are about twelve vacancies per unit at this rank.

The next rank is Sergeant, once you have held the rank of Corporal for three years and have passed an education course which consists of maths, English, leadership and management. The management course was one of the worst ones I have ever done. It teaches the theory, some of it useful but most of it dreamt up by someone who has not even been a soldier. You have many group discussions. On our course there were lots of Royal Military Police who talked rubbish and had no idea what happened in a soldiering environment. Myself and two paras had a big argument with them and we were taken into the teacher's office (the same office where there was that scandal when Captain Crumpet was all over the Sun newspaper for having sex over the desk with a sergeant on one of the education courses). We were told that if we did not change our attitude we would be kicked off the course. We spent the next three weeks being very quiet and listened to what we thought was rubbish. We got split up and had to sit away from each other in the classroom.

They teach you the theory behind leadership, but in my opinion you have either got it or not. Some people just know how to handle people and have a certain 'X' factor: they inspire others and have a certain personality that makes you want to listen and be near them. Some people have just not got it, cannot communicate and are damn right boring. I remembering asking someone a question and after two hours where I wanted to strangle myself I got away from him and slept for two days. Some people just lack that certain 'X' factor. If you ask me what it is I could not say but you certainly know when you come across someone in command who has it.

There are about eleven Sergeant vacancies per unit. At this rank you will carry on doing the job as you held as a Corporal, and then later move up to Troop Sergeant, where you are in charge of about thirty men with a Lieutenant or Captain above you. You also move in to the Sergeants' Mess which in my opinion is one of the best clubs to be part of. Every member has proved himself and has earned the right to be there. To reach this rank is an excellent achievement; some do it in eight years, while most achieve it in about ten to fifteen years. Once you have got to this rank your status in the regiment goes up rapidly and even the most miserable arrogant officer normally talks to you with respect. One of the most important jobs of the Sergeant is to educate and keep his young officer on track (they come out of Sandhurst and have a lot to learn). I think that they don't normally really know what they're doing until they reach Captain and have at least five years' experience under their belt. It is at this rank that you could get posted to other regiments in other units to fill in vacancies and you normally got posted away for a couple of years to gain further skills.

The next promotion is to Staff Sergeant. Usually there was one vacancy per unit, the requirement is that you complete more education courses and have three years' experience as a Sergeant. It is at this point you get vetted from outside your unit. It's not just the case that your Commanding Officer thinks you're good and promotes you, all the reports from all the other Sergeants in the Corps go around a table. A selection of other Commanding Officers and Brigadiers mark and score your reports and the top few get the promotion. You are therefore competing against everybody in the Corps (that could consist of twelve thousand men). It is only a small percentage that actually passes the promotion board and earns the job. At this stage it all depends on how good a report writer your Commanding Officer is. You could be the best soldier in the world but if it is not put into words, then you will not score the points. The system is fair and there is no way that someone who is on the board can ostracise you, if someone does dislike you, they cannot discriminate against you. If any individual scores more than two points of anybody else then they have to score it again until everyone has scored the report within two marks of highest score to lowest. These boards only sit once a year.

After Staff Sergeant you are then promoted to Warrant Officer, Class Two. You will first be the Troop Sergeant Major in charge of around thirty men, and then the Unit Sergeant Major, in charge of about one hundred men.

There is another board you must pass to achieve unit Sergeant Major, with this role you are the top soldier in a unit of about one hundred men and at this rank you receive a Royal Warrant from the Queen. Once you have made it to Warrant Officer Class Two it is then promotion to Warrant Officer Class One, the selection is done on the same procedure, but there are only around eleven vacancies in the Corps for Regimental Sergeant Major, and about ten other Warrant Officer Class One slots a year. On promotion to Warrant Officer Class One you will be the top soldier in a regiment of about five hundred men so to actually make it is quite an achievement.

In my opinion, during your career you will come across someone who does not like you, they may try finishing your career or just make your life a damn misery. Thankfully when this happened to me the person in question was only my CO for three months before he left, and my career was saved. If he had stayed I know I would not have made it any further up the promotion ladder as my reports by him would have not been good enough.

I was very lucky to make the grade as I never found the technical stuff easy and had to spend hours reading my books to learn and be able to compete with the others, however, those who could just listen once, take it in and do no extra work and then score a hundred percent in exams were not as gifted as I was with the management of men. I had to work hard just to equal them technically but I always achieved results when it came to the soldiers under my command, this was mainly due to common sense and pure determination. The higher the rank you achieved the higher the standard of competition. On the whole the promotion system works and the ones who are lucky enough to make it to the rank are good, you do get yes men who are only interested in their career, these I'm sorry to say I despise, but apart from that the men who do make it are very talented, there are those who don't who are equally able, but just did not make it due to being in the wrong place at the wrong time.

CHAPTER SIX

War

After three years as a Lance Bombardier I was promoted to Bombardier and put in charge of an M1O9 155mm self-propelled gun. These guns were capable of firing a ninety pound shell over a distance of eighteen miles with a variety of different ammunition such as high explosive shells that on explosion would spread shrapnel over a distance of 180 metres, killing those in the path of it. These could be set to burst in the air, this was used if you had soldiers in the open with no protection, or set to go off underneath the ground (for example, if soldiers were dug in a trench system), or on impact with the ground. These shells were also used to fire directly at tanks. We could also fire smoke shells, to give a good smoke screen for our troops, either to help them advance, or to retreat without being seen. It could also drop either anti-personnel or anti-armour bomb mines. The anti-armour would explode on contact with an armoured vehicle, and the anti-personnel if someone stood on it. Also we could fire white phosphorus that would burn on contact with the air, setting light to whatever it came in contact with. I felt like a real grown up and it was definitely where the real responsibility began. I was in charge of multi-million pound equipment and six men, in war time this number would increase to twelve (the main difference was that I was the sole person in charge and if there was a mistake, I was responsible). My drills had to be spot on; if I made a technical mistake it could lead to some one dying. This was put to the test when I went to Canada on live firing training exercises. The British had use of a training area out there which was basically hundreds of miles of prairie, just the same as you see on a Cowboy and Indian film. The area we trained on used to be the home of the Blackfoot Indian tribe. The reason we had to go to Canada was because there was no training area in England that could match the size of the one in Canada. The whole Battle Group deploys together and trains in as close to war conditions as possible, this is where you have the tank regiments, infantry, engineers, air corps and artillery all training together. These exercises are fast-paced with live ammunition, as close to war conditions you can get, there are plenty of accidents and sadly sometimes casualties. My battery lost one man on this exercise. He was trapped against a vehicle by a 24 tonne gun, and his body was nearly cut in half. After his death the battery was put on parade and given fifteen minutes to think about what had happened, mourn him, and then told to get back on with the exercise and crack on with the job. (There's a monument outside the training establishment in Canada and it is filled with names of soldiers who lost their lives on these exercises.) There are lots of safety precautions but when you have armour driving at night with no lights, live ammunition being fired, things are bound to go wrong. Also there are mistakes that are inevitable due to tiredness and the wrong drills being carried out. On a number of occasions rounds landed where they shouldn't, which lead to casualties. Even if there were no casualties, if mistakes were made soldiers and officers were sacked and their careers were ended. If the battery was on a fire mission and the order 'Detachment, rear!' came over the radio, everyone in a command position's stomach sunk, this normally meant that there had been a mistake. On the receipt of this order the gun crew would leave the inside of the gun and would stand behind it. You weren't allowed to touch anything, especially the gun sight. The Gunnery team would then appear on the position and would check the command post; this was to see if their drills and maths were correct, they then would check the gun sights to make sure that the correct bearings and elevations had been ordered by the command post and had been applied to the gun sights. If this was correct they would then check that the correct ammunition had been fired. You might wonder why mistakes happen after all the training that a soldier does. All I can say is imagine sitting in a small room, bearings and elevations being sent down your head sets, different ammunition orders, gun crew shouting and loading shells, a big engine running loud, the temperature inside the room around 35 degrees or minus 5 and you've only had six hours' sleep in three days. The figures you take down are passed on to another man who applies them to the gun sights. This is all done at a fast pace. These were the conditions we were up against; it is a credit to the army that these mistakes happen so rarely. Consequences can be horrendous. I remember on one occasion when mistakes did occur, but luckily no-one was killed. One case was a young officer, he had made a mistake in the Command Post and the guns had fired on the wrong data. He'd input this data so was responsible. He was told to put all his equipment on and to make his way to the Commanding Officer's position on foot, which was five miles away. On his arrival the Commanding Officer told the RSM to drill him in front of the other members of the regiment. After being humiliated and made a fool like this he was put on Commanding Officer's orders and fined. Being on exercise was boring sometimes, there was a lot of sitting around doing very little, but you must remember that when war is on it is not everybody fighting at the same time, so you will get rest times. Having said this, on a fast-paced exercise it is extremely hard work. There are six men living off your vehicle and the work is physically hard; you could deploy to different positions up to eight times a day. Each time you deploy you have to bring the gun into action, prepare, move the ammunition, dig trenches, pack and unpack the kit. This is not done at a slow pace, it's done with every man doing everything at double speed, and sometimes you live on two hours' sleep a day. The weather can be snow, rain or heat, you were either sweating from the heat or freezing with the cold. As well as this you have to stay mentally alert to carry out the technical drills required of you. You don't get to wash properly, so you all stink, your clothes smell of gun powder, sweat and dirt. Whilst on sentry, standing in a trench with the rain pouring on you, wet clothes stuck to your skin, fighting to keep your eyes open, you had to stay alert as you were the eyes and ears for the position and everyone in the unit's lives are in your hands. When the rest of the unit are asleep their lives are in the hands of the men on sentry stood in a trench at two in the morning with the raining coming down and fighting to keep your eyes open if they are not alert then everyone asleep could be killed very easily. You possibly would get off sentry at two in the morning, but knew you had to be up again at four to start again (you tried to get sleep in your wet clothes). After days of this you still had to perform as though you were fresh and full of beans, when you drove on long night moves in the pitch black with no lights on it was difficult to stay awake and to stop your head from dropping. There were times that you were so tired that you started to imagine things were in front of you when they were not. Our main role was to fire the guns to support our infantry and tanks. We also had to defend our gun positions, this meant digging of trenches and manning them as well as manning the guns. Our fire power was good; we had the six 155mm guns plus the six machine guns on the turrets, as well as our personal weapons and anti-tank weapons. If we were attacked we could put up a good fight, we had around one hundred men and about sixty vehicles, and this is exercise at its worse. You train hard for war so when it comes you are ready for the reality of the conflict and you are prepared well. Lots of soldiers say they love exercise and hate being in camp, I cannot say I hated it but certainly did not love it. On this particular exercise a soldier was bitten by a black widow spider. He was having a toilet break when he was bitten on the backside. He went blind for three days and spent a week recovering in hospital. There were hundreds of these spiders every-where and you had to be on your guard so that you did not become one of their victims. You would often see men running around like lunatics trying to brush these spiders off their equipment. There were also lots of rattle snakes around. I used to hate walking through the prairie at night, never knowing when a rattler was going to introduce himself to me.

It was at the end of one of these exercises that Saddam Hussein, with his 100,000 Iraqi troops, invaded Kuwait. The Kuwaiti forces were unable to defend themselves and Saddam Hussein had seized this rich oil state. The first rumours started that we might be involved in some sort of conflict (at no stage did I think we would be involved and did not take any notice of the rumours that were flying around).

On return to Germany the regiment was put on parade and the Commanding Officer told us we were deploying to Saudi Arabia with the Americans. For once the rumours had been true and at last we were going to be given a chance to put the years of training into action and do what we had all joined up to do, fight and protect! I had served eight years and had no medals on my chest as the only operational theatre was in Northern Ireland and I had not had the chance to serve there. Nowadays you see soldiers with a rack of medals on their chest as the British Army has been involved in the Gulf, Bosnia, Kosovo, Gulf 2 and Afghanistan. Little did I know then that within seven more years I would have five medals. We were lucky as our Brigade was the one who had finished its training cycle and was operational ready to be deployed. From that point on the Regiment turned into a war footing. We were issued with desert rat badges to wear on our arms, which I believe was because the press back home was making a big fuss of the desert rat thing (the original desert rats had fought against Rommel in the desert in the Second World War). The first thing to happen was that the Regiment's man power was increased to a war establishment (about double that of peace time; these people came from the regiments that were not being deployed). We were always short of manpower, we were supposed to be able to man six gun crews and two command posts, but it was often the case that we would only deploy on exercise with four guns and one command post due to not having enough men. With the eight guns and the two command posts and all the support vehicles, there are about seventy vehicles per sub unit: a lot of man power is needed to support all of these. If the whole Army was deploying then these numbers would come from the Territorial Army and reservists (these are people who have left the Forces but can still be called up for emergencies). They would be called and then put through a period of refresher training; my six man crew was now twelve men. With the gun I was also in charge of two Ammunition Vehicles, these we had to borrow off the Americans, they had track vehicles (our ammunition vehicles were wheeled and would have got stuck in the sand and not been able to keep up with the guns). I was twenty five, my second in command was twenty three and the average age of the rest of my crew was nineteen. We were young, fit, highly trained young men ready to deploy to a desert that we knew nothing about; we were ready to take on an enemy that was supposed to be capable of putting up a treacherous fight, they had lots of fighting experience and had used chemical weapons on previous enemies. We were all keen to go and excited at being given the chance to do what we had joined up for. You often hear people saying our troops should not go to these places but most soldiers want to go and those who weren't usually did everything to get attached to a unit that was.

I can't explain the excitement I felt at being told we were going to the desert with a good chance of seeing action. There were a couple of instances of soldiers from other units refusing to get on the plane because they were scared and did not want to go (in mine and lots of other people's opinion these people should not have joined in the first place). When the time came to show what they were made of, they were found lacking in courage; luckily these incidences were quite rare. I can understand being scared once under fire but being too scared to even go to the conflict? That I can't understand. The other batteries replaced their Bombardier Gun Detachment Commanders with Sergeants from other units; I thought this was bad drills; their argument was that they wanted men with more experience in charge; the Bombardiers were well pissed off. They had been in charge and now they had the chance to command in a war situation, that chance was taken away from them. Sometimes officers flapped and didn't look after the men who had served them well so far. Our battery did not take this route and the Bombardier number ones remained in charge of their equipment. This was our Battery Commander and his Battery Sergeant Major having faith in his men. I would have been gutted if they had taken my gun off me and given it to someone else. The six guns per battery became eight guns per battery with the crews being made up of men from other regiments; all sorts of equipment began to arrive. On our gun turrets we had a General Purpose Machine Gun; we were issued 50 calibre machine guns to replace these. These had been kept in a store somewhere only to be used in a conflict, the only problem was that no-one knew how to use them and we had to get the Americans to teach us (this was rather embarrassing). All sorts of equipment arrived, we should have had it in peace time really but as we were going to war there and then it was decided to give the equipment to us to actually use. The Regiment then went on full time training, we had to concentrate on fitness and nuclear biological chemical drills as this was seen as a major threat to us. They had used nerve agents on a village, killing five thousand people, many women and children, so the threat was real. If an army uses chemical weapons on civilians, it tells us a lot about them. It made me even more eager to get on and stick it to them. There is lots of administration to do as well, such as writing your will so your loved ones are looked after in the event of death. The Army has a form to fill in: you put who you want things to be left to, you sign it and that's your loved ones taken care of if you die. You are issued your dog tags which you must wear round your neck at all times, these have your name and number on and are classed the same as your ID card: if you lose them you get charged, these are used to identify you if you have the unspeakable unfortunate experience of being killed. There is a good chance your body will be unrecognisable and the dog tags might be the only way of knowing whose body it is. You suddenly find yourself outside the medical room with your arm getting used as a dart board with all sorts of injections. If you can catch it then you are injected against it. You basically walk through a line with different people putting different needles in you. The dentist then takes an x-ray of your mouth. I think this is used to identify you if the rest of your body is blown to bits. The sort of injuries in war that you may incur are not always small bullet wounds, they are more likely to be complete destruction of the body from burning or explosions.

The Regiment then has a mass of briefings about the Iraqi Army, these briefings gave us the impression that we were up against a formidable opponent. They were experienced in war and had special regiments such as the Republican Guard. These men had been fighting in wars for years and were classed as their elite forces. When the war started we would be fighting them, but at this stage nobody knew this as the battle plans had not yet been formed. We spent a long time learning what types of equipment they had and how to recognise them, this was very important as you don't want to fire on your own troops in mistake, or think the enemy are your troops and don't fire on them until too late. The equipment was then sprayed a desert colour and we were all ready to deploy. The Regiment went on one more live firing exercise where we were given more ammunition to fire (we now had more than we would in three years of training). These rounds weigh ninety six pounds and you can have up to five hundred on one position, which you have to manhandle around. I remember on one fire mission we had sixty shells to fire, if you think that a shell cost around one thousand pounds, and that there were twenty four guns … firing this amount of ammunition was a lot of tax payers' money going down the range, but it is worth making sure that the men the country sends to fight for them are as well trained as they possibly could be and also have the best equipment they could have. The Army has invested a lot of time, effort and money into equipment for its soldiers and is probably getting it right now; this preparation went on for about six weeks. The equipment was sent to Saudi Arabia with about a dozen men, these men had a good trip on a ship sailing down the Nile, jammy beggars but they did say most of the sailors on the ship were gay and they spent most of their time keeping their backsides out of sight. The Captain told them they should not walk around in their shorts as his sailors were getting uncontrollable. We drove the vehicles to the local railway sidings; the same one as the Jews had arrived at to go to the concentration camp at Belson, probably the most famous ones were Anne Frank and her family. We loaded them and off they went; we all flew out a few days later. We arrived at the local airfield which was parked full of military fighters. I had never seen so many military aircraft all in one place. We then drove to the port in Saudi Arabia. The port was full of men and equipment, we were to stay there and get used to the heat then get the equipment prepared before deploying in the desert. Everyone was put into big warehouse buildings where you slept and waited for the equipment to arrive. Living in these conditions were horrid, men farting and snoring, luckily we did not have to stay there for long. For ten days more men arrived, when the whole Regiment was at the port waiting for the ship to arrive with the equipment. We were anxious and apprehensive but we were ready to get on with job in hand. The ship finally arrived and we got the guns off it. We parked our guns in one long line on the dock, with the rest of the battle group's vehicles. Guns, tanks and all sorts of armoured vehicles, a whole Battle Group; it was a very impressive sight. There were lots of American ships in the docks; they were loading masses of equipment. Their soldiers were all trying to get hold of our gas masks (as ours were a lot better than theirs and would offer all sorts to try and get them). We would often swap rations with each other so we had a variation in what we ate; it was at this stage that people started to go down with the runs. When you queued up for your food you were in long lines and the food was outside with hundreds of flies. We were told if you get the shits it was self-inflicted, they said this was due to bad hygiene, but if you get that many people in those conditions and heat, things like that will happen. Every night we had an evening briefing, the commanders told us that a soldier had been evacuated to England because he had dysentery and we were told if we got it, we would well and truly be in the shit, literally! That night one of my mates said he was feeling bad I had no sympathy for him and took the piss called him a poof and went to bed. When I awoke in the morning I felt terrible and started to use the toilet every ten minutes, I was being violently sick and couldn't eat a thing; this went on for three days.

The runs you have in these conditions are unbelievable; twenty times worse than the normal dosage you would have had back home. I can't explain it but I think the feeling you got from it was not much worse than you could be on your death bed. I managed to hide it from everyone bar my gun crew who helped me hide in a tent. My Second in Command went to the briefings at night and made some excuse for me, this was accepted as it is often the case that the Second in Command stands in for his Commander (we did have people in this position who felt like as a leader they could not let anyone be trusted apart from themselves). It is good to give those under you the responsibility, it makes them feel good and it is all part of their education, in this environment where there is a good chance of being killed or wounded, the Second in Command would have to perform your duties. There are times you have to sleep and he will definitely have to be in charge. It got to the stage where I had to be helped to the toilet because I was so weak. The toilets were portaloos. If you can imagine a battle group of soldiers using these things, you can imagine what they smelt like, especially in the heat of Saudi Arabia. I was that weak from going to the toilet about twenty times a day that I could only just get my trousers up and down, I have never felt weakness like it before. The problem was that I was so sick that I did not want to go and get treated, in case I was sent home like the soldier I had heard about on the briefing. It was bad because I could have passed it on but there were lots of people doing the same as I was, it just had to be done. We had a regimental parade where the Commanding Officer gave us his final words as a Regiment before we deployed in the desert. This would be the last time the Regiment would all be together until after the war had finished. I had to stand through forty

118

five minutes of this with my Second in Command, one of the gunners holding me up, with poo running down my leg. Even though I felt like death I had to pretend I was fine, the next day the Regiment left the docks and deployed to the desert to carry out crew training under the Gun Commanders. I was standing in my turret being held up by two members of my crew, as I drove past my Battery Commander I saluted him and once out of sight fell down and slept in the back of the gun, my Second in Command carried out the crew training, luckily that day the bug went and I started to feel better. I am pretty sure I had dysentery or the nearest thing to it. This was the first day of six months that we were to live in the desert living off our guns (our tanks). The guns were now our mobile homes and we were self-sufficient. We carried everything we needed to survive from our personal kit to ammunition, food, water and fuel. The guns were fully bombed up with war stocks of ammunition. This included all the artillery ammunition that consisted of the different shells and the charge bags to give the explosive force to fire the shells. As well as this we had all our personal ammunition and personal weapons. This consisted of bullets for our machine gun and rifles and grenades. For the next two months we trained and trained and then trained a little bit more and once we finished training we then trained again.

From a soldier's point of view it was great to be in the desert, just you and your gun crew living together, having laughs and playing practical jokes on one another. Lots more men and equipment were arriving daily, whilst a political solution was trying to be reached by the world leaders. There was a major threat from Saddam using chemical warfare against us. He had used it before so we had to take a tablet three times a day which was to help protect you against nerve agent poisoning. These tablets had to be taken daily and they had some bad effects on some poor individuals. Basically you were putting nerve agent in to your body three times a day. I remember watching a sergeant roll about on the ground twitching and being sick, pooing himself after taken one (he was suffering from nerve agent poisoning). The effects did not last for long, all those around him had a great time laughing at him, the laughs we had sometimes come across quite cruel but the whole aim of a team is to get through what you have to, it's the best camaraderie I have ever experienced and probably ever will. I think the nervous tension gave the atmosphere a tense one but also a one of survival and hilarity at the extent of the circumstances we were put under and were in. We seemed to have loads more jabs, one of which was the anthrax jab which made your arm feel like Mike Tyson had been using it as a punching bag. The pain lasted for about two days (a few soldiers refused to have the injection as it had not been used before). There had been a lot in the press about Gulf War syndrome and the possible effects of the cocktail of injections. As yet I am fine and I don't know anyone who I served with as being ill. On return from the desert I did suddenly develop an allergy to something which gave me cold symptoms for about three weeks at a time; it was as though someone had put pepper up my nose. This lasted for about four years and wasn't a pleasant experience but didn't seem to have any ongoing long lasting effects. I don't know if the peppered nose was related to the Gulf but you never do know. My dick did shrink by two inches; this, I tell women, was due to Gulf War syndrome. It must have been the injections.

One calm night during a break of the constant exercise we were all sitting on the front of the gun, just as it was turning from day to night. A couple of the lads tied a piece of string to a scarf and dragged it so it would look like a snake. We were all in on the trick so we didn't get scared (I guess the boredom or sick kind of humour sometimes got the better of us), but one poor lad, not quite sure how he drew the short straw, was bellowed at that there was a snake, we all tried throwing him into the path, but he was having none of it, understandably as they can be poisonous. He was only a little man but he grabbed the gun barrel for his dear life and would not let go. It is astounding how strong people can be when they are scared. Six of us could not drag him off the gun barrel.

Unfortunately during all the training and exercises another soldier was killed, he was crushed by one of the guns which weighed in at twenty four tonnes, yet another soldier to give the ultimate sacrifice for his country.

We had arrived in October and had been living in our vehicles, training and getting used to desert conditions. After two months of constant exercises, the equipment and personnel were extremely worn out so we were given a week's rest over the Christmas period. Before we knew it, it was Christmas Eve. The battery all ended up together in a quarry to have Christmas celebrations. On the night of Christmas Eve I had just got in to my sleeping bag, when I heard gun fire, about five shots and shouts of stand to (this is where you deploy to your all round defensive position to defend against an enemy attack). This is a well-rehearsed drill with every member of the team knowing where he has to go and his arcs of fire. This is important, especially at night as you don't want people shooting your own men. The trenches are manned and the machine gun on the turret also. The gun turrets are manned so the guns can fire 90 pound high explosive shells in the direct role (this is basically where you fire at a target you can see; the indirect role is where you fire at a target you can't see, up to eighteen miles away). I thought 'Bloody hell, what a time to start the fighting, on Christmas Eve!' I then caught on pretty quickly how clever it was, as it would have caught a lot of people off their guards. I made sure my crew were in their positions and told them to load their weapons ready to fire. There was then a strange silence with all the battery in their trenches and firing positions. Here we were, one hundred and fifty of England's young trained men all in position to do their bit and make their name in the history books ... and it was all a farce, orders were given to stand down. Disappointed as we were, we obeyed orders. The Commanders were called to the Command Post for a briefing where we were told what had happened. We were told that one of our soldiers had tried to put some bullets in to the Battery Commander's Land Rover where he was sleeping. The reason being was that he had some problems with his wife back home and the Battery Commander would not let him home to sort it out. So in anger he had shot his rifle at the Battery Commander's vehicle. Not sure if he wanted to kill him or if he was just trying to get noticed, well it worked, he was flown back days later and we never saw him again. On the whole, the Army is brilliant when it comes to compassionate situations and soldiers are normally looked after, especially when it comes to their families, I know that civilian companies would not look after their work force in the same way that the Army looks after theirs.

Christmas day was spent with a big dinner, and opening parcels from people at home which was really appreciated, little things in the desert where there is not a lot to occupy you can mean such a lot. It wasn't nice being away from family, especially children, at these times, but a job is a job and we all cracked on with Christmas and made the most of our mates. The people back home were brilliant and we got hundreds of parcels with hundreds of letters, food, sweets etc., these were from our loved ones and people we didn't know. Someone sent us some cheese and pickled onions. It was amazing how good they tasted as we hadn't had that sort of food for so long. During our time in the desert there was no alcohol so we celebrated with fizzy drinks (it's a good job I wasn't a drinker as I think this would have been difficult if I had been). Once we saw the New Year in, we deployed on more training exercises.

We were given three days where we were sent back to a camp in Saudi Arabia. The accommodation we were put in had previously been used to house refugees and the dirty bastards had wiped shit on the walls that we had to clean before we slept in them. That was quite revolting. We were adopted by ex pats living in Saudi for a day, and they fed us and gave us showers. It was nice just to be out of the desert for three days, but like all good things, that came to an end and we were sent back into the desert. One night we were sent to a camp where the medics put on a show for us. The standard of entertainment was fantastic and I could not believe how much talent the medical corps had, from singers to bands to plays, it was great. The main star was Spit the Dog who had flown over from England. It was funny when he asked if anybody had a lighter and all the soldiers chucked them at him at once. Unfortunately one hit Bob in the head and nearly knocked him out, he came back on with blood rushing from his head and all bandaged up, he did see the funny side and said admittedly you shouldn't ask a group of soldiers something like that if you don't want a cascade of them.

The hardest thing about the desert is map reading as there aren't any road signs, it's just sand and the odd feature; it became a fine art. On one occasion I broke down and once the REME (Royal Electrical and Mechanical Engineer) had repaired my gun I had to travel twenty miles to find my battery. As it was getting dark and I was lost, I had no idea where I was. Luckily I bumped in to a American officer who showed me where to go. I was only about half a mile from my battery so had nearly made it. He had a GPS; we did not have them in those days. As I hit the gun position my BSM came up to me saying, 'Good to see your map reading is up to standard!'

'Yes, it's basic skills, Sir,' I replied feebly. My Second in Command was trying not to laugh as five minutes before I was completely lost in the desert at night, staring at my map, thinking 'Where the fuck am I?' This is not a good thing but I am not afraid to admit it is a skill to navigate in the desert with just a map and compass, which takes time and practice to learn.

The other thing that you had to look out for was old lakes that had dried up. If you went over them in a twenty-four tonne armoured vehicle, you would stop and sink. This happened to one Commander and I remember seeing him standing to attention with the Commanding Officer going mental at him.

It was on one of these exercises that we were doing a night move and had stopped for ten minutes, some of the lads got outside for a stretch and a pee, the order came down to move again. I shouted in to the turret,

'Is everyone in?' and a reply came back,

'Yes, everyone in!' I told the driver to move, and on hitting the gun position I shouted,

'Halt action spades!' This was the signal for the gun crew to jump out and bring the gun into action. There was a deadly silence. Then the back door opened and out jumped one of my crew.

'Where are the others?' I asked angrily.

'We have left them at another position,' he replied worriedly.

I went mental because he had told me they had got back in. At night when it is pitch black you cannot see into the turret so rely on the senior crew member to tell you that the crew are all in. About five minutes later my crew turned up. They had been picked up by another vehicle. The section commander who picked them up was laughing his head off, especially when he saw how angry I was. It could have turned out to be an embarrassing incident and I would have been well and truly in trouble if someone had found out that I had lost seven men from my gun crew. I made the Gunner's life a misery for days, to make sure they were aware of the seriousness of the mistake that had happened. I do admit if I want to be I can be a right b****** and for some reason that incident really annoyed me and I soaked for about three days.

On one exercise we had deployed onto the position and were just carrying out some dry firing exercises (this is where you do everything apart from firing the ammunition; it's a safe and cheap way to train) when all of a sudden over the radio headsets there was an outburst,

'Whose gun is on fire?'

On hearing this I popped my head out of the gun turret and immediately noticed that about one hundred and fifty metres to my left was a gun on fire. I could see the flames popping out of the two hatches; the gun crew was stood around the gun, making attempts to put the fire out. It is bad enough when you have a twenty four tonne armoured vehicle on fire but when it is fully loaded with complete war stocks of ammunition (explosive shells can cause shrapnel to ping around over one hundred and eighty metres), tearing to bits anything they hit it is particularly dangerous. There was smoke, shells, a mixture of normal smoke and white phosphorus, which burns when in contact with the air, and bomblet shells. These shells were made up of armoured and personnel bomblets, as well as the thirty plus artillery shells. There were also the charge bags that basically are big bags of gun powder that are placed in the gun barrel behind the shell, they give the explosive force to propel the shell on to the target. There was also a mass of hand grenades and all the small arms bullets that go with the personal weapons and the machine guns. It was a massive amount of explosives confined in what was basically a metal tin with a gun barrel sticking out of it. All of this was just waiting to cause a massive and deadly explosion. The flames started to get bigger and the 50 calibre machine gun on the top of the turret started to pop out bullets all around the position, the heat had set it off. A 50 calibre bullet is about six inches long and about one inch wide, so if you are hit by one of them you are more than likely to be killed. At this stage the gun crew started to run for cover and then there was a massive explosion. All the ammunition had exploded at once, the gun exploded into lots of small pieces, sending chunks of metal over one hundred metres in to the sky. The explosion was so powerful that I was knocked from my turret hatch down on to the turret floor. My gun crew were thrown off their feet and there was a loud thud as a piece of metal crashed into the side of my turret. Our bergans, carrying our personal kit, had been hanging on the outside of the turret. These were peppered with shrapnel and were left smouldering from the heat. There was shrapnel and metal flying all around the position with about one hundred and fifty men lying around the gun positions trying to shelter from the lethal, deadly metal. At this point the ammunition vehicle that was parked behind the gun also caught fire; these were tracked vehicles that the army borrowed from the Americans (before that the ammunition vehicles were big wheeled lorries but these were no use in the desert trying to keep up with armoured track guns as they would get stuck). The ammunition vehicle carried over seventy more shells of various styles and also exploded, sending even more metal shooting over the position. There was then a sudden silence. Where the two vehicles had been there was nothing left apart from the odd bit of metal and tracks. All around the position there were metal, pieces of ammunition and unexploded bomblets. The only place there were not pieces of metal was where a body had been taking shelter, to this day I don't know how anybody did not get hurt or killed. The muzzle brake, which is the part on the end of the barrel and weighed over three hundred and fifty pounds, was found over three quarters of a mile away so you can imagine how powerful the blast was to send something that heavy over such a far distance. Three American apache gunships had seen the explosion from seven miles away and turned up on the position, hovering overhead. They thought there had been some sort of battle and had come to investigate and lend a hand if we were being attacked. The gun crew from the gun were standing in a group, obviously in a serious state of shock. We were then ordered to move to another position, so we moved off and were redeployed (the gun and ammunition vehicle were replaced within two days). We were told that a wire had sparked and burnt through one of the charge bag containers and had caused the fire. There were rumours that someone had been smoking in the back of the gun or had been using the cooker, however it is only the gun crew who will ever know the truth. Three days later we were on an orders group and we saw another gun from another battery explode in the distance, we didn't know the story behind that one but the Army had lost two artillery guns before the war had even started.

At this stage we kept up the constant training, we had been on exercise for three months (we were the first to deploy in October, most of the other troops did not deploy until after Christmas). A long night move had just finished and we stopped before we deployed to our positions. I climbed down from my turret and said to my driver,

'I'm getting some warmth from the engine decks and shutting my eyes, wake me up when we move.'

We often did this, we took it in turns to get five minutes (we were not at war yet and we had had about five hours sleep over two days). Unfortunately he fell asleep as well, the next moment I was being woken by the RSM screaming at me, he told me I was in the shit and to report to my BSM when we got back to camp. I got in my turret and told my driver he was a twat for dropping me in it. I spent the next two hours a very worried man as it was the Badge who had caught me, so I knew I was going to be punished.

When I got back to camp I looked for the BSM. I found him with two other gun commanders, they were standing to attention getting wasted, and he looked at me and shouted,

'Not you as well?'

'Yep,' I replied, trying to give my sorriest face I could manage. With that I found myself next to the other two getting a nice bollocking in the desert. The BSM used to say, 'Come with me for a walk in the desert!' and when he said this you knew nothing good was going to happen, only punishment. It turned out the other two had done the same, I've never been so chuffed to see those two scoundrels. We all got ten extra guard duties; I think that was us getting off lightly. This was a good result as the Badge could have put us on orders in front of the CO but he let the BSM deal with it as he had thought our corner. On one of these extra duties we had to burn all the waste from the toilets that we used in one of the fixed positions. We had to empty all the poo into black bags and burn it. Not a pleasant experience, it got everywhere and we ended up covered in it, so maybe we didn't get off so lightly after all.

Two soldiers from another unit were on sentry in a trench when a large poisonous snake decided to slip into their trench to join them for a chat. The soldiers were not too keen on the idea and jumped out of the trench screaming. There were also scorpions around but they seemed to stay away from humans. One night I got into my sleeping bag and felt something run over my head fast. I think it was a lizard but I did not sleep well that night. We were not allowed to sleep on the guns or inside the turrets as if a fire mission was called for, the last thing you would want would be bodies and equipment slowing down the speed you can fire the shells on to the enemy, so we all slept outside under a shelter. Inside the turret there was always one man manning the radio and machine gun. You could be asleep and within a minute you could be in the turret firing on the enemy.

We used to listen to the radio and the Iraqis used a women to broadcast, she was saying (or should I say droning),

'You are all going to die, go home, your girlfriends and loved ones are shagging about, why are you here? Go home, no-one cares about you.'

We used to find it funny listening to her ranting as though it made any difference to us. We nicknamed her Baghdad Betty. On one of my extra duties I was based at the command post when it came over the radio that the air war had started. At last we were close to being unleashed and allowed to do the business on the Iraqis. All day and night we would watch the aircraft flying over us to carry out their missions, on one occasion we were told they were going to drop massive bombs that night on to enemy positions that weren't far away from us; I think they were ten thousand pounders. I was on sentry in my turret manning the radio and the machine gun at about two in the morning when there were massive explosions and the night dark turned to daylight. The explosions were like fireworks you'd never imagined, I would not have liked to have been on the receiving end of them. Every day we used to watch the aeroplanes flying over us to bomb their targets. It seemed to go on all day and night. Around about this time we were told that an Iraqi (calling himself Captain Bond) was pretending to be a British Captain and had been seen five miles from our position. We were told to be on the lookout for him at night time. I must admit that when I was standing in the turret that night my head was turning side to side, panicking that 'Captain Bond' was going to come behind me and slit my neck.

We were redeployed to our fighting positions, the guns were taken by tank transporters and we were given a ride by the Royal Air Force, who kindly dropped us off five miles in the wrong place, the twats. They have navigation aids so there was no excuse for it. In fact it was very poor and slack drills but whilst they were back in their hotel enjoying a drink around their pool we were walking across the desert with all our kit. When I say our kit that is, your webbing that has your ammunition, survival kit etc. in it, your rifle, helmet, and your bergan, so all in all about eighty pounds in weight. A young officer realised their mistake, how I don't know, as it was just one mass of sand to me, but due to his map reading skills he got us to where we should have been. After walking five miles with all our kit in the desert, the two pilots who dropped us off were not on our Christmas lists.

We were going to be attached to the American division. The British had most of their artillery guns deployed (about seventy two guns), while just this one American division had around five hundred guns. This shows how massive the American Army is compared with our own.

It was good when all the training stopped and we were poised for action. The padre seemed to appear on the position the entire time, great if you were into that, but on the other hand a pain if you were not. Church parades in the desert became regular; my gun crew tried everything to get out of them and even volunteered for guard so they didn't have to go. I always stayed behind to do the guard and sent my crew off to hear the padre go on. One gun commander once asked the padre to bless his gun; this is where I must point out that the only gun to get blown up was the one blessed by the padre (as you can guess I'm not a religion fan, just another of my strong opinions). Once I was on a fire mission, we were firing in our gas masks, which is very unpleasant, especially in the heat of the desert, and the padre poked his head into my turret and shouted out,

'Good to be here!' With that the reply he got was,

'Fuck off, it's not! And get away from my gun!'

It wasn't what he was expecting and walked off looking very shocked, I'm not sure what else he was expecting as I was busy concentrating on the firing. I was revved up on the fire mission and controlling my crew. He reported me to my Battery Commander and I had to explain my treatment of the padre. I explained the circumstances and he smiled. I'm sure he must have been thinking fancy him popping his head around the corner and saying it was a nice day when we were firing shells and possibly killing people.

We spent about three weeks in a fixed position with the guns dug in and spread about over a distance of a mile; it was a pain having to walk the distance three times a day for orders at the command post. You were not allowed to use torches at night for obvious reasons, although I used to see torch lights being used all the time, especially when the gun commanders were called to the command post for briefing. It was the snakes that put the fear into people, you knew they were there and were scared to walk around in the pitch black in case they bit you, in which case you'd be in a lot of trouble. Other regiments were given the chance to go on gun raids and fire on the enemy and we had to sit and watch them drive past us. This was not good for our morale as we had been the first regiment to deploy in the desert and it looked like we were going to be the last to fire the guns in anger. Also we had to watch the rocket launches pull around our positions, fire on to the enemy and then drive off.

The commanders were called to an orders group and we were told that the next day we were deploying on a gun raid. We all cheered as at last our day had come. This was where we drove to the border, fired on enemy positions and got out of there as quickly as possible before the enemy returned fire on us. When I returned back to the crew and told them the news the air was full of excitement as at long last we were going to put all the training into practice and fire on the enemy. That night I did not sleep much due to the excitement that was ahead of us the next day. It was like being a child going to sleep on Christmas Eve, waiting for the morning to come so you could open your presents. At last morning did come and the guns were lined up in position and the order to move came. The members of the battery who were left behind on the gun position all cheered us off.

After travelling about five miles we arrived at the firing position. The order 'Tiger!' came over the radio, which was the order to deploy, and I deployed my gun into its firing position. The gun crew was so revved up I remember laughing, watching all these young men running around like gladiators fighting for their lives (unusual response to our situation, again, but it seemed to happen a lot). Within seconds the fire mission came over the radio and we fired fifteen rounds of high explosive shells onto the enemy. It was great; the crew was so revved up, the ninety six pound shells were getting thrown around as though they weighed nothing. I was finding it so hard not to laugh at my loaders as I never seen them so hyped up. We fired our rounds on three Iraqi positions. Later we were told that we had done significant damage. Imagine twenty four guns firing fifteen rounds each on to a target; it would not be nice to be on the receiving end. I looked through my gun sight and to my amazement I saw Kate Adie doing a news report, I thought this was strange, especially as we could have received incoming fire. Once you fire the guns, the enemy can pick your position up on the radar and then return fire on to you. The order Cease fire!' came over the radio and we got out of there as fast as we could. Kate Adie stayed there filming us. Maybe she knew something we didn't but she was in no hurry to get out of there.

That was our first taste of the action, my gun crew of young men had done their bit for Queen and country. It was only a quick action but the morale was high as we came back to the gun position, all proud of what we had done. One of the guns had broken down just before the raid so they could not go on it, they were well pissed off. Of course we took the piss out of them and called them cowards and that they had broken their gun on purpose because they were scared, this wasn't true it was just sheer bad luck. My father, who was back in England, was in the operations room as he was a serving RAF officer. He saw our regiment being moved off the operations map and asked what had happened to us, but they couldn't tell him. It was a worrying time for him as my brother was the gun commander of the gun next to me, so he had both of his sons serving in the desert in the same unit. It made me laugh when he told me he got stick from my mother who constantly told him he should be out there not her sons. He was relieved when the regiment was put back on the map after we had finished the gun raid.

During this time we were treated like film stars with the press and film crews trying to get as many interviews and film shots of us. I remember I was told that my gun was going to be used on the BBC, that they would actually filming a piece in front of my gun. When the recording started I walked to the front of the gun to see what it would have looked like. The gun was dug in to a gun pit with big rocks all around it to give it more protection but to my horror I looked down and there was a freshly laid human turd with rolls of used paper. One, this is bad soldiering, as it should have been done further from the gun where we lived, and two, it should have been dug into the ground and buried. I went back to the crew and acted as a mad man trying to find out who the phantom pooer was, of course no-one owned up to it and they tried blaming it on the film crew. Somehow I couldn't see Kate Adie leaving one after she had filmed her report, so knew it was the crew. I had nightmares about it being on the ten o'clock news and all you would see was this big turd lying there.

The commanders were called for to an orders group that didn't finish until two in the morning, it was one of those where people ask stupid questions just for the sake of having their own voice heard. I got back from it and jumped in my sleeping bag in desperate need of sleep as my ears were hurting from listening to pointless crap all evening.

When a missile flew over our position a lot of people started to put the gas mask on as this is the drill, it could have been a chemical attack, and the warning went out, 'Gas, gas gas!' I was so tired I did something really stupid. I turned over in my sleeping bag and said, 'Fuck it, if it's time to die then let's get on with it.'

This was incredibly poor soldiering but I was so shattered. Later we found out it was one of our own locating missiles returning after filming some enemy positions.

On another occasion we had another chemical alert. This time I did take it seriously as the scuds were being fired by the Iraqis. We were in our guns, in full protective suits and gas masks. My crew was asked to carry out a sniff test, this is where three of you go outside and remove your mask to see if there are any gases still around. This is not a great job if there are; if the poor sod who has to take off his mask finds out there is still gas there, he could be seriously affected. The commander has to stand by, watch and be ready to give first aid. I went outside with two men and could see that the locals were working in the quarry next to us and were not suffering, so I gave the order 'Gas clear'. My crew looked at me as though I was really brave; they had no idea that I had seen all the locals working fine. We always seemed to be in and out of our gas masks due to the scuds being fired by the Iraqis, and also as our detection equipment around the position kept going off. It was always a false alarm.

Practical jokes were rife in the army and especially if you had time on your hands. If an opportunity arose the first to recognise it would take it quickly. Once we all ganged up and waited until one of the lads was having a strip wash, we waited until he was naked with soap in his eyes, then we all put our gas masks on and hid his and started to scream, 'Gas, gas, gas!' (this means there has been a chemical attack and you have nine seconds to put your gas mask on). It was hilarious for us onlookers to watch him run around naked with soap in his eyes trying to find his mask. We all were shouting,

'You're gonna die, get your bloody mask on you fool!'

He found it funny later, but initially the shock shut him up. Another of the crews did an even worse trick, one of them put a turd in a gas mask and when the victim tried to put it on, his body was a sight, I must be honest I am so glad I wasn't on the receiving end of that one. Another was done because a chef had been pissed off by an BSM, he put a turd in the tea urn that was sent out to

136

the ranges. Everyone was complaining about the tea and when the BSM looked in he saw the turd bopping up and down. This was a joke too far and the chef got a sentence in jail for it. There were a lot of wild dogs in the desert and on one of our positions there were three puppies who kept howling at night as there was no sign of their mother. The BSM gave the word for the puppies to be killed. This really upset a lot of the Battery, strange as the men were there to kill the enemy and wouldn't think twice about it – but innocent dogs? That's a different matter.

About a week passed when the commanders were called to another Orders group. We were told that this was it; the ground war was starting tomorrow and that it was time for us to go in. We all cheered. We were given our orders and timings and were given a good speech by the BC and BSM, who told us what they expected from us, and that they knew that we would not let them down. We had to go back and brief our gun crews. When I got back at my gun pit I got the crew together and told them, 'This is it lads, we are going in to Iraq tomorrow,' and briefed them that we would start at five in the morning. I passed on all the information that I had that we were going in to Iraq to fight the Republican Guard, and then we were going to swing into Kuwait. The Republican Guard was their elite fighting force. I made them do their final battle preparations such as checking their equipment and cleaning their rifles, etc. I personally checked their gas mask and protective clothing as once we were moving there was no chance of sorting it out. I made sure the machine gun on the turret had clean ammunition and was ready to fire. I then told the Non-Commissioned Officers to stay behind and told them that we didn't know what we are facing, and that I was relying on them to help me get the younger lads through whatever lay ahead. I had spent nearly five months in the desert living off my gun, for some reason I knew that it was going to be a fast moving battle and we would travel miles. If you broke down you could get left behind so I stocked up on food supplies (one week's extra rations). I didn't want to be in the desert, on my own, hungry. I was going to fight an army; I had no respect for them as a whole. I always had the view that they were strong when they were in the dominant situation but weak when they came across someone who could fight back, plus they were rumoured to be bum bandits and I had no intention of allowing myself to be captured and finding out if that was true. All this animosity towards the way they lived made me really look forward to getting stuck in to them. I would have done whatever it took to make sure they were not going to get hold of my backside. I wasn't scared, I was full of excitement and truly believed I was doing a good job by following my duties. I knew my crew was well trained and I could rely on them to get stuck in and do whatever was going to be asked of them. Loads of British soldiers had done all of this before and would do after we had our turn. I knew that in any situation that lay ahead I could rely on those twelve men to watch my back, as they could rely on me to watch theirs. It is not until now that I look back at that time that I realise how lucky I was to be given a chance to be in that situation. Many soldiers have served but never been in combat. I was lucky: I was in the right place at the right time.

Two of the young lads showed signs of being nervous. This was understandable, we reassured them that they would be fine and there was nothing to worry about. It was inevitable that a few of the soldiers would wind them up by telling them that there was a good chance of them being killed, and how great the Republican Guard was, but seriously we did all re-assure each other to say that there was nothing to worry about. But in my head I knew the unspeakable consequences of us being out here, we were going in to an environment where people would be killed. I had faith in our training, equipment and skills, and rest assured we were fine. We all tried to get some sleep, apart from the sentries. Since October we had been on exercise and done twenty four hour guards (this meant the gun turret machine gun and radio set had to be manned, plus the trenches that were dug), so we were getting an average of four hours sleep per night. Everyone had to be awake at first light for stand to, so by now we were tired, but we were so excited about the thought of actually going in and doing the job and getting home. It's all a bit unreal and you start to have the attitude that nothing is going to happen to you. This surreal unrealistic thinking I had to nip in the bud to make sure I didn't let myself or my team get complacent about the consequences: if we were blasé we'd make mistakes. Stick to your training, judge your instincts (such as when you just get that feeling something is not right) and you should be ok. Of course there are things that you can't stop and if it's your turn then that's the way it is. This was our job and I reminded my men and myself that we were fighting for our country and our lives and when the time came it is kill or be killed. I also reminded them that it was everyone's responsibility to watch each other's backs, and our lives were in each other's hands.

About three o'clock I was awoken by the sentry, I was pissed off as I had only just got to sleep and was expecting to be in my sleeping bag for another hour. It was raining heavily, it was damp and cold, and it had just come over the radio, 'All commanders to the Command Post!' The weather was not like I thought the desert would be. It was cold at night and either raining, or sandstorms with the odd hot bits. At the Command Post where everything was happening at a very fast pace we were briefed that the timelines had been brought forward and we were crossing the border now. This was a good sign as it showed the battle was going better than expected already. Even though it had got me out of my sleeping bag early the first signs were that maybe the enemy were not going to put up a good fight. I had just got back to my gun crew and was about to brief them when the order to move came over our radio. We started into battle. All the vehicles of the battery were moving in fighting formation across the desert. It was a great sight to see. Each mile we were getting closer to the enemy who were waiting to try and stop us. We came to the border which was marshalled by RMPs (Royal Military Police), showing they did have a use apart from arresting drunken soldiers. There was a big tank burn (where the sand has been piled up to make a barrier to stop you getting through in to Iraq), and a route had been made through it. The minefield had been cleared for us to be able to travel through it. We travelled a few miles into Iraq and I passed two of our tanks that had broken down. The commanders were well pissed off as they were missing the action. This would have been my worst nightmare, breaking down and missing everything. We crossed the tank burn as it was just getting light. It was still raining. We travelled about two miles into Iraq; all the time I was alert, scanning everything in front of me as now the enemy could be anywhere waiting to kill me. If any of them showed themselves then I was going to make sure they got a burst of my 50 calibre machine gun before they had chance to attack me or my crew. Whilst on the move the crew are in the gun and the only defence was me on the machine gun, so their lives were in my hands. Then the order 'Tiger!' came over the radio; this was the code to deploy off the line of march and into action. The gun crew were sitting in the back and couldn't see anything that was going on, at least the driver, the second in command and I, could see, our heads stuck out of the turret. I gave the order, 'Action!' to my crew and they started their well-rehearsed routine of bringing the gun in to action. Within seconds a fire mission came down and we were firing on the enemy; eight guns from the battery were firing on to enemy positions. Fifteen rounds were fired and in a matter of minutes the order was given to cease firing and we were on the move again. This had all happened in minutes. Yet again the guns were in formation and clouds of sand were being thrown in to the air as the guns travelled towards the enemy. We drove onto an enemy position that had been totally destroyed, all the vehicles were on fire but there were no signs of any bodies. I found this a little strange and to this day still don't know where the dead people's bodies went. It makes me think that maybe they had run away and left their equipment.

The same happened again. As soon as we had brought the guns into action, another fire mission came in and we started firing on to another enemy position; we stayed on these targets for a long time, firing about forty rounds each. To the rear of the position there was a loud explosion. I looked out of the gun turret to see what it was, and there was a loud shout from the Battery Sergeant Major.

'Face your fronts!' he screamed, 'there is going to be plenty more of that before the war is over!' I never did find out what the explosion was. I know that a lot of the trench systems were booby trapped, so maybe it was one of them going off. My second in command shouted,

'Do you want me to take over and you have a rest? This we did but I was soon to realise why he was so keen to get in to the back of the turret. When I got outside of the gun I was hit by a massive sand storm that had appeared from nowhere (these storms are extremely unpleasant: the sand hits your face like gravel being chucked in it). It gets in your eyes and mouth and makes your face sore and itchy later on. The storm lasted about five hours. The git had taken me for a ride, so I decided I'd check next time before agreeing to swap jobs with someone. The order 'Cease fire!' came down and off we went again. During the storm we were constantly in action, firing against the enemy. It was much of the same for the next two days, long moves, deployed and fired on to the enemy. We carried out a very long night move; I remember seeing an enemy compound surrounded by British tanks, blasting it for hours (whatever they were firing at, I would have not liked to be in it). Whilst driving at night you have little idea of what lies ahead of you, so you have to be as alert as you can. At least in daylight you can see far ahead. We did have night vision aids but nine out of ten of them did not work and were of no use.

On the morning of the second day we deployed on a position just as light was coming up, the guns were in a straight line and the crews were sorting out their administration, getting washed and cooking breakfast, when a message came over the radio saying,

'Take post!'

This meant that everyone had to stop what they were doing and take up their positions of action. There had been reports of an enemy trench system around three hundred metres in front of us, and someone had seen some Iraqi soldiers jumping into it. We found out later on there were three hundred Iraqi soldiers in it. If they had been good they would have taken us out before we knew they were there, it would have been easy for them to blow the guns up with their anti-tank weapons. The gun barrels started to swing on to the enemy position; my second in command was manning the 50 calibre machine gun on top of the turret and I was looking through the gun sight, trying to see the target. All eight gun commanders were onto the Command Post asking for permission to open fire but it came down as wait. My crew were really revved up for action and we were all full of excitement, at this stage a mass of British tanks and six helicopters arrived on both flanks, ready to join and attack. The sight of the tanks must have been too much for the enemy, the white flag was shown and the three hundred of them surrendered. I then told my gun crew to stand down. They went mental, kicking things and swearing and shouting,

'This is so wrong, why did they not let us fight?'

They were so revved up to fight the enemy and were seconds from it when it was taken away from them. There was no fear in them, just excitement and eagerness to do their bit for their country and their regiment. The reason we did not know the Iraqis were there was because we had deployed at night in the pitch black. It was a fast moving battle so things like this happened. It could have been worse and we could have deployed on top of them. That would have been a nightmare with a lot of deaths on both sides.

The enemy was rounded up and taken away on transport vehicles. This showed us that when they were against weak opponents they were keen to fight, but against a well-trained force (who would have fought until they died), they did not want to know, and once again this knocked any respect I had for them, for being cowards.

It was around this stage that the sky started to turn black from the oil wells that had been set alight hundreds of miles away. The black sky was with us for the rest of the war, it is one of the things I vividly see in my mind on a regular basis. From then onwards it was the same thing, driving long distances, deploying, firing a few rounds and driving again. The main problem was that we constantly had to be refuelled, the distances we were travelling were long and we nearly ran out at one stage. On one of these moves we passed a burnt out vehicle. To the side of it I could see half a leg with the boot pointing upwards, about ten metres from that was a pile of someone's insides, the best way to describe it was that it looked like a pile of sausages left on a butcher's table. Then I passed some more burnt out vehicles. Inside them were two bodies that were completely black; they looked like a sausage that had been over cooked on a BBQ. We started to pass more and more burnt out vehicles and had a stream of the enemy walking past us, who had surrendered. On one occasion I must have had some pity in me as I threw a tin of rations at them. It was ok for me to live this life with this as my job as I saw their evil ways, for some people who are all good and see the good in everyone it would have been a lot more difficult, and increasingly so as the war continued. When I threw the food they all dived on the ground and started screaming for their lives, they must have thought I had thrown a hand grenade at them. I was pissing myself with laughter. After that every time I passed the enemy who were surrendering I chucked them a tin of food and it kept having the same effect with them diving for cover.

It kept me entertained and also gave them some food, so we were all winners. It did cross my mind later that they might not have a tin opener.

Once again we deployed on to another position and this time a tank alert came over the radio. My brother's gun crew had seen an enemy tank coming in our direction. On the order 'Tank alert!' we took up a direct fire role, basically we fight as though we are tanks, yet again one of our tanks took the target out and that was the end of that. We were ordered a fire mission on what was suspected to be an enemy recce platoon. It was night time and the OP (Observation Post) was not sure of the target, he thought it could have been one of our own troops but we were loaded ready to fire. It was found to be our troops and the fire mission was cancelled (they came very close to being fired on by their own guns), a good example of troops using their initiative and not being too gung-ho and just firing on anything.

My mate told me about his father who had been in the Lancaster's in the Second World War and had a lot of experience. Ten years later (I think it was in Kenya), he was ordered to take his squadron and take out an enemy patrol, as he flew over the target he could see the patrol but realised they were not trying to take cover. He used his initiative and ordered the mission to be cancelled; it was later to be found that it was a friendly patrol. If he had been less experienced and not able to think on his feet, he could have killed a lot of our own men. As you can imagine this is how tragic scenarios can come about, the seriousness is not apparent amongst the soldiers visually, but if you were to ask them seriously about this stuff they would answer very clearly about the dangers and accidents that can easily happen. We then did a long night move and deployed on to another position, we were told that two British vehicles had been taken out by American aircraft and a number of British troops had been killed by friendly fire; this meant we were required to fly union Jacks from our vehicles to help identify us. As well as this we had bright orange panels on top of the turrets so aircraft could see we were on their side. Unfortunately for the onlookers and the owner, the only Union Jack we had was a set of boxer shorts. They belonged to one of my crew, so they spent the rest of the war on the top of the turret of the gun. Even more unfortunately for him (and me), he had used the boxers so his skid-marked boxers would be now flying off my radio aerial, about one metre from my face.

We spent four days on long moves and firing on the enemy. The sky was constantly black from where they had set light to the oil wells; daytime was black and night time was even darker. Long moves, fire missions on the enemy were basically what we did.

Out of the blue it came over the radio that the enemy had surrendered and the war was over, it had been a short war and the enemy had been pathetic. The only thing I was bothered about was I'd done my job and my men had accomplished theirs. We had fired over three hundred rounds on the enemy on time and at the right place and had done considerable damage. I know that if the enemy had been more willing to fight, my crew would have fought until the last man was standing. Spending six months in the desert with my crew; being left alone to soldier is an experience, unless you have done this you would never understand the camaraderie and bond that goes with young men in this environment. My gun crew was ordered to drive off to headquarters to be met and congratulated by the Prime Minister. On the way there we past hundreds of burnt out vehicles. It was where the enemy had tried to escape but had been blasted by our forces. My crew was met by John Major who was the Prime Minister at the time. He told us how proud the country was of our efforts and to get home and enjoy our leave. We spent about three more weeks in the desert until we drove our guns to the docks, then we were sent home and were given six weeks' leave.

The army somehow lost my gun, no-one knew what had happened to it but we kept getting reports that had been sighted in England, this went on until it finally arrived back, unfortunately this was five days before we were going to deploy on another exercise. (It took over four months to turn back up at our camp. The rest of the regiment's equipment had arrived safely within six weeks.) I thought I was going to miss the exercise, just about everything had been stolen including our personal things, some twat that had not been in the war had stolen our stuff, whoever it was I'd just like to say they're scum. This new exercise turned out to be the hardest we had ever done. This was because we had a new Commanding Officer who hadn't been in the war. I think he had a point to prove as his opening words were,

'Ok, you been to war as a Regiment. Now you're back and you are mine for two years.'

After the war I received a commendation for my work in the desert, I'm not really sure why, I guessed it was for just doing the job well (most of the Gun Commanders were Sergeants and I was a Bombardier with a lot less experience). My commendation was as follows:

> Bombardier A. Topham, serving with the
> Divisional Artillery Group 1st Armoured
> Division is commended for meritorious
> services during operation Granby and the

battle to free Kuwait, Operation Desert
Storm in Saudi Arabia, Iraq and Kuwait in
January and February 1991.

The experience of the desert and war is one that I feel
honoured and lucky to have had; it was a privilege to be
part of a well-trained unit doing what they had trained
to do for so long. The privilege too of being in charge of
twelve young men, all different personalities and characters, is something that will stay with me for life.

CHAPTER SEVEN

Climbing the promotion ladder

After a six week leave where I put on a stone and a half in weight and could not fit into my uniform, I was called a fat bastard by my Troop Sergeant Major. To my satisfaction most of the soldiers had done the same, they'd spent their leave drinking, eating, and slobbed out on their arses. I have to admit after spending six months in the desert and then having six weeks' leave I was not looking forward to being back at work and doing the normal routines, exercises and duties again. When you are in an environment of doing hard exercise all week it is amazing how much weight the body puts on once you relax for a few months and stop the exercise.

Our equipment was returned from the Gulf. After six months in the desert and on constant exercise it was all a bit battered so we had to spend a lot of time maintaining it and getting back to mint condition. It was all painted green and black again and we started the routine of exercises. The Regiment was then put on alert for Bosnia and the guns were painted white, I was well pleased that we were going to be given another chance to go and do the business on another enemy. We were all ready to deploy again for another six months' tour and another conflict. I thought this was great as I had had so much fun on the previous operational tour. As far as I was concerned, this would be more of the same and far better thing than hanging around camp. We went through the same procedure as we had for the Gulf, briefings and training; the only difference was we were training for cold conditions and a terrain of mountains, not the heat and sand of the desert. One of the officers had a contact with the Americans who managed to get us all warm winter boots at the cost of one hundred pounds. This hurt, having to splash the cash out but the thought of my feet freezing in Bosnia was not a good one. Unfortunately we were stood down and never went. But on one occasion the guns were all lined up ready to move so we got very close to it. I was well pissed off and asked if I could return my boots and get my one hundred pounds back but was told to piss off. I must admit they come in handy now when I go fishing in winter. For some reason the government decided it was not the time to send in troops, this was a shame as it was the beginning of the Balkans War, there was a lot of fighting to be done but we missed out on it. A year later they did send in troops but unfortunately it was a different battle group and we missed out on it again. After the Gulf War one of the soldiers had told people that he had been a hero and made up some stories on how he had single handed taken out loads of the enemy. This story was put in his local papers; unknown to him at the time, one of our soldiers saw it and gave it to the BSM. The battery was put on parade and the BSM read out the article from the paper. The soldier concerned was dying with embarrassment, it was his own fault, he shouldn't have bullshitted the people back home. I often find that the people who have been through some real action don't talk about it. They then made him march out and presented him with a bravery medal. It was made out of tin foil and he had to wear it everywhere he went, it was hilarious and I think the humiliation would have stopped anyone else repeating such lies.

They held a big conference in Bournemouth to talk about the Gulf War, all the top ranking officers and every RSM were there to listen for three days. Myself and a Sergeant were chosen from my regiment to go and talk about our experience; we were flown back to England and spent three days in a 5 star hotel on Bournemouth beach. There were big screens and about six hundred people at the event. All the other regiments had their Commanding Officers and RSMs speaking, they all looked at us a bit strange to see it was just a Sergeant and a Bombardier speaking for our regiment. We had a ten minute slot; all the other regiments did their bit and I must admit I was falling asleep myself, never mind anyone else, they were all very serious and boring. Our turn came and from the first second we started we had the audience laughing and at the end got a standing applause, the Commanding Officer who had spoken before us looked at us with embarrassment as we had definitely impressed the congregation. I must admit when I was at school as a boy I was always playing the class fool, and always had the attention instead of the teachers, it didn't do me so well at school as we were supposed to be quiet and learn. I remember once the teacher said a rude word and me and my friend fell off our chairs laughing, we were already at the front of the class, so she could keep an eye on us. I work with the same mate now four times a year on motor shows, and I really like to have banter. On return to the regiment we were told to report to the Commanding Officer urgently. My BSM said,

'What have you two twats done? The CO wants you now!'

We were marched in and his first words were,

'What the hell did you two say at the event?' He then started smiling and said, 'Well done, my phone has not stopped ringing with everyone from the Brigadier and every Commanding Officer saying what a great job you'd done.'

We were still at our base in Germany and life continued pretty much as normal, with the odd incident here and there. I remember around about this time one of the lads met a girl. She told him she was seventeen and one thing led to another and they had sex. It turned out that she was fifteen, though. Her mother found out about it and the poor lad was arrested by the German police. He spent six months in prison for it. Another time, a local girl was raped, they caught the man but ten of us who looked like him had to go on an identity parade. I had to stand next to him and could just make out the women looking through the glass; I thought that with my luck she would pick me. When the parade began I was very worried because it looked like she was staring at me. When put in that situation you automatically feel guilty, however unbeknown to me I was actually right next to her attacker. He did get picked out and I believe he got a long sentence. I must point out he was not a soldier but a local German lad.

At this time some soldiers played a joke on a new officer. They tied him to the garage doors, six foot in the air, and left him there over the lunch break. It was light hearted and the officer took it in fun as it was meant, and did not mind. He did mention it to his father, though, who was a serving Brigadier and did not have such a good sense of humour. The soldiers all were sent on orders and were demoted by one rank. Around about this time another young soldier from the regiment lost his life when the vehicle he was commanding turned over and crushed him to death. Also just outside the camp a tank over turned into a stream and the commander could hear his driver on the radio drowning as the water was slowly entering his driving compartment. The commander could do nothing to help him as the man was trapped and he couldn't get to him. He could just hear him screaming for someone to help. I'm glad I wasn't ever in a position like that; it must have angered and upset him to not be able to help in any way whatsoever.

Another soldier was killed when he did what you were not allowed to do: he fell asleep underneath his armoured vehicle. The vehicle sank into the ground whilst the soldier was asleep underneath it and he was squashed to death.

For the next five years I started to climb the promotion ladder. I was promoted to Sergeant after passing education courses and proving myself as a Gun Commander in peace and war. This is a big leap in the promotion world, you escalate from a Junior Non-Commissioned Officer to a Senior Non-Commissioned Officer. The responsibility you have is greater but the respect you receive from all ranks makes the most noticeable difference. The pay was a prominent factor in this promotion as it starts to get a lot better. The only pain about it was that you had to buy your own Mess Dress uniform, which you wear for functions and dinner nights, and sets you back about four hundred pounds, incidentally if you put on weight (as you do as you get older) it can get very expensive.

Around about this time people started to join who had been brought up with drugs and there was a lot more thieving and random drug testing. The testing team would appear with no prior warning, the gates would be locked and no-one was to leave the camp. Everyone had to pee in a bottle and if proven positive, the individual was kicked out, there was no messing about. I was all up for this as I had had a non-drugs upbringing and didn't want drugs coming in the Army. I think there would normally be around four to six soldiers who would have positive results, I must point out they were always the private soldiers who had not been in the Army long, they were quickly found out if they were messing with illegal substances. You can't have soldiers dealing with live ammunition who have taken or who are taking drugs. There is a story of an American fighter pilot who was a drug addict. He got away with it until he had a flash back whilst flying. He ejected from his plane for no reason. On one test I was standing next to an officer who told the team,

'I pee twice a day: once in the morning and once at night.'

It was funny watching him standing there all day drinking water but true to his word he did not pee until late at night. Once a bombardier came up to me and said he smelt drugs in one of the rooms. I reported it and the four lads were kicked out as soon as it was proven to be true. Apparently the local drug gang was going to sort myself and the bombardier out but nothing came of that.

I stayed with my regiment for three more years, doing the same routine of exercises. We went to Denmark on an exchange visit with the Danish Army and one night we had a games night and they wanted to take us on at tug of war. They were big strong lads and all looked like Vikings, so we tied one end of the rope to a truck outside the tent so they couldn't see it and we put our smallest men on the rope. They couldn't believe it when they couldn't move our lads and we won, they were so shocked that these small men were so strong. We were pissing ourselves with laughter. Whilst in Denmark we were told that a bar called the Spunk Bar was out of bounds, the BSM said there was trouble there. I think every soldier from the Battery managed to get a picture of themselves under the bar's name (including the BSM). If you tell soldiers not to go somewhere they were more likely to go and seek the place out, they would let their curiosity get the better of them, they wanted to know what they were not allowed to see or do.

We went to Italy on an exchange. The Italian army were strange, we watched them walking around holding hands. I think the Italian's regimental march is one where they march backwards, they not known as the best army in the world. We did play football against them and got slaughtered; they had two professional players who whenever they kicked the ball it went into the back of the net. I think it was thirteen nil, not much difference from our international team. Whilst in Italy one of our lads did not have any money so he went to a gay bar and let them chat him up all night to get free beer, another soldier from another regiment tried this but was found lying unconscious in the road with his trousers down to his ankles; only he will know what happened that night.

The IRA started to kill soldiers in Germany so you were alert all the time, checking your cars for bombs. The security on camp was tightened up. There were a number of attacks on solders in Germany and quite a few were killed, either shot or blown up, the bridges on the roads used to have pictures of bombs exploding with the words, 'You next' on it. Our cars had special number plates that told everyone you were British, but these were later changed to match the German ones. I remember a black

BMW pulled alongside me, it had blacked out windows and stayed with me for ten miles, driving directly beside me. I thought I was going to be the next victim as this was how they had killed some soldiers. The terrorist cell was caught by some Dutch farmers who stumbled across them when the IRA was testing their weapons in the woods. The farmers took them on with their shotguns and called the police. They were very brave for doing that and saved a number of soldiers' lives. One of the cell members was a woman. I drove through a crossing two weeks before the IRA team was waiting for a British car to turn up; they were waiting at the traffic lights so when the car with British number plates was stopped by the red light, they put two bullets in the car, killing the RAF serviceman and his small daughter. I could not help wondering if they were there when I had driven through two weeks earlier. During that time I took the ferry home, two weeks later it was sunk, killing lots of people at Zeebrugge (I seemed to be missing everything by two weeks). Around that time a lad got caught thieving, he thought he'd got away with it as he was leaving the Army anyway, but two hours before he got on his plane he received a good kicking from all the soldiers he had thieved off; they stole his money back for compensation.

I spent my time still as a Gun Sergeant Commander and had a small stint at the Troop Sergeant role. I had been on the guns now for ten years and a Gun Commander for five years. After having the privilege to fire my gun in anger I was now getting bored of the routine of exercises and was ready for a change. On my very last fire mission I nearly made a mistake that could have led to the round landing in the wrong place. Luckily I noticed the mistake seconds before I fired but this showed me I was getting tired and needed a break from gunnery.

My duties as a Sergeant were of all descriptions. One duty was as the Duty Orderly Sergeant, which you did once a month. One of the tasks when carrying out this duty was to close the bar on camp at 23:30hrs. The only problem was it was the night that the Welsh Guards had just returned from a hard six month tour of Northern Ireland. I had to go there with four men from the guard, armed with pick axes, and three military policemen, who had three guard dogs with them. I entered the bar and shouted 'Last orders lads please, drink up and leave in ten minutes!'

I was met with a chorus of,

'Fuck off you Gunner twat, we are going nowhere!'

The problem was solved by me sending in the dogs with the military police men. The drunken soldiers soon sobered up and left with no more trouble, but believe me it was a scary experience having to tell a regiment of drunken soldiers to stop drinking and go home.

Normally around this time of your career you are posted away from your regiment to gain experience doing a different job and to give you a break from regimental life. I was sent on four instructor courses so I could be an instructor at a training depot, these are high profile postings that can either destroy or make your career. One of the courses you have to do is the All Arms Drill Instructor's course. You get beasted from the moment you wake up and to the moment you go to bed. The course is run by Guardsman. They are a strange breed who think life revolves around drill and not much else. My drill was crap but I managed to scrape through. If you are five foot eight you just don't look as good as a six foot Guardsman in his best uniform (I must admit the Guardsman I came across were more concerned about bullshit and drill and not interested in soldiering), but these were drill instructors and I can't believe the whole of the Guards Regiment are like that. I then had to do a skill at arms course so I was able to run a shooting range and teach the recruits different weapons. This qualification made me instructor in all infantry weapons Also I did the first aid instructor course and the nuclear biological chemical instructor's course. Whilst I was on the first aid course one of the female students had to do a lesson on how to give mouth to mouth resuscitation using a doll, one of the male students waited for her to go out of the classroom then wiped his penis all around the lips of the doll, of course when she started her lesson and then demonstrated the mouth to mouth resuscitation we were in fits of laughter and she could not understand why. To give her credit, when she found out about it later she had a good giggle about it. When I was on the nuclear biological course you spent most of the three weeks in a gas mask. Once I had to pretend I was a casualty and was put in a body bag for thirty minutes. It was the most horrid experience I have had. I just wanted to rip the mask off so I could breathe but was not allowed as we were supposed to be in a chemical environment.

I spent twenty four weeks on courses just to get the qualifications to enable me to teach the new soldiers. I arrived at Pirbright and was told I was taking over my troop. The only problem was that the Officer, Troop Sergeant and four Bombardiers had all been sacked; they had gone drinking with the recruits whilst adventure training and some of them had got into a fight with them. Lots of people were sacked due to over-stepping the mark with the recruits, you had to be so careful when dealing with them, and nowadays you can be sacked very quickly if one makes a complaint against you which is upheld. I did get a new officer who was one of the funniest and best officers that I had the privilege to serve with. I also had some good bombardiers and this was the best two years I served in the army. It was great fun and you achieved a great sense of achievement watching muppets walk through the gate, and then turning them into good soldiers. Only approximately eighteen out of thirty would make it. I had one recruit who tried to commit suicide. He was just trying to get attention more than really killing himself. I was more concerned about the blood he had dripped over the carpet rather than him slitting his wrist. In the end he sorted himself out and made it as a soldier. The recruits had a sense of humour earlier on in their career. I remember during adventure training one time when I was getting in to bed at night, the little darlings had taken all the bolts out so it collapsed when I got in. I found it funny and did not say anything about it, but must admit the morning run was two miles longer and at a much faster pace just so they knew that I was the boss. My regiment did a tour of Northern Ireland when I was at the training depot so I missed out on that one. I did twenty three years' service but never did a tour of Northern Ireland, you could say that was a lucky escape. I did well here and was promoted to Staff Sergeant. I was told I had to go and do a year-long course, where you learn about every piece of equipment in the Artillery. I really did not want to do this and the thought of being in the classroom was horrible. I tried to get out of it but was told I had to do it if I wanted to make it up the promotion ladder. The weekend before I started the course I decided to go and spend a couple of days with a mate from Civilian Street who is a bit of a hard bastard. I ended up in a pub with him he said,

'I am glad you come to see me, I am meeting three lads who want me to do some of the security down the south coast.'

They were three gangsters who had operations around the country and heard my mate was the man to talk to before trying to move in on the south coast. They turned up; one had just left Spain (due to the Russians moving in) as he had had a shot gun put to his head on four different occasions so decided it was time to get out of there. He was built like a tank with shoulders the size of a house so I could not imagine who would have had the guts to put a shotgun to his head. He was one of the men who appeared in the book *The Governor*. The other two looked like complete nutters and not the sort of men that you would mess with. My mate did his business with them and they ran the security on the south coast. A year later they had an argument and my mate ended up beating them up; a conflicting situation which ended up in a brawl. They asked me if I would like to work for them, doing security for the rich and famous, I said thanks for the offer but not for me, they said that I had something about me that would be ideal for those roles. They liked to have people who did not look like thugs, but men who just blended in but could look after themselves. I was not going to go down that line. On this occasion my mate took me to a club and we were escorted through to the VIP lounge, due to his fame in the area. In all the other pubs we had been in, not once did we have to buy a drink. We had been in the club about half an hour when my mate came back from the toilets with blood on his shirt. I said,

'What you been up to?'

He said that five lads had started on him in the toilet so he had gave them a good kicking. I didn't believe him so went to have a look, true to his word five lads were being carried out and were in a mess. The night went on and I started to notice groups of lads staring at us, suddenly a group came up to me and said,

'You got five minutes to get away as your mate is going to get a kicking by some gypsies.'

My mate had been surrounded by another group; it was one of those situations where you had to think fast, so I shouted to the bouncers,

'Get us out of here!'

Four of them got us out of the VIP entrance, and as we got outside it was like a scene from a western; at least sixty of them followed me and my mate.

'Back to back we take as many as we can,' my mate said.

Six of them ran at us, one hit my mate who just stood there laughing at them. There was a taxi five metres away so I dragged my mate into it and got out of there fast, he was pissed off as he wanted to fight them. He kept shouting,

'You changed! You're not the man you used to be!'

There are times when the number against you is too much and it's best just to run.

The next morning he was complaining of a bad foot, so I took him to A and E. It was found he had a broken ankle; he had missed one of the lads in the toilets and had hit the toilet instead, breaking his ankle. It was not a total disaster though as he managed to get a date with the nurse who treated him.

I then had to go on a one-year technical course, this was the worst year and I really didn't want to do it but had to in order to get up the promotion ladder. I knew it was going to be bad on the first day when a mathematics professor came in to teach us the maths theory behind gunnery. He used two sides of the blackboard to do the first sum and he might as well been speaking in Latin as I never understood a thing. I had two scuffles with two other students on the course. They were complete twats and spoke to every one like they were worthless. One of them had a go at me, he was a big lad and thought this 5ft 8 quiet boy was an easy target. He ended up keeping his hands in his pockets as I was told him I was going to break every bone in his body. He turned out to be one of these who give it large but back down when scared. Another did it in the gun turret and I ended up pinning him to the corner, this was another one who backed down. It was the first time that I had met some real arseholes who did not care about anything apart from their career; some of them were real horrible people. I struggled on this course as you had to learn every drill and every bit of equipment in the Artillery. You spent four weeks on one subject and then moved on to the other, by the end of the year my head was scrambled and could not remember anything about the first half of it. I scraped through but at the end my head was a blur and I could remember very little. If a subject normally took six weeks to learn, we had only three weeks to do it, and then moved on to the next one; difficult unless you were a total Tefal head. My brain could get scrambled. I am someone who needs to be shown and then practise something before it sinks in. I cannot be filled with loads of information and not put it into practice. I really had to work so hard just to get through the course. We had to go up in the helicopters and learn Air OP (Observation Post) work, the pilots thought it was great fun to go as low and as fast as possible, twisting in and out of the hills. I was sick for the whole thirty minutes we were in there. Whilst on the course, some of the students left for

162

a day to attend a soldier's funeral from their regiment. He was shot in Northern Ireland by the Armagh Sniper. He was standing at a checkpoint when he was hit. The sniper used to lie in the back of a car and fire a 50 calibre rifle through a small slit in the boot of the car. He was responsible for a number of soldiers' deaths.

After that year I was promoted to Warrant Officer Class Two and was posted to a TA (Territorial Army) Regiment, this I loved. I found that they were good lads who finished work and then played soldiers at the weekend. I had to do a lecture to the regiment at the end; I asked if there were any questions and a Staff Sergeant said,

'Yes mate, I have one.'

I had to educate the TA that if you're below me you call me sir, if you're higher than me call me Sergeant Major. I was not their mate! It reminded me of an RSM who was taking the officers for drill. He shouted to them,

'I will call you sir; you will call me sir; the only difference is you mean it!'

They're really civilians and need to be reminded that when they are playing soldiers, they have to abide by regular army rules. One of the soldiers we called Trigger, he was just like the one off 'Only Fools and Horses'. On one exercise the CO held a conference in a pub. We were round a big table when Trigger entered the room with a beer in his hands and said,

'Hey, what's going on here, can I join you?'

The reply he got from the RSM wasn't probably what he'd hoped for:

'Fuck off out of here you twat!'

A regular soldier would have not dared to go within a hundred meters of a Commanding Officer's Orders group. I was crying with laughter and tears running down my cheeks, trying not to show it too much. The

RSM kicked me under the table to stop laughing. We had a great Regimental Sergeant Major there and it made the posting real fun. A lot of the officers were pants as they were only doing it for the social life and used it as a club. You do get some old eccentric officers; I came across one when my mate had to book a training area for the TA to use on the weekend. He phoned the officer in charge and made the booking and told my mate that when he arrived at the gate, he had to press the button and say into speaker, 'The milk bottles are empty,' and he would be let in. Two months later my mate went down to the camp the night before the TA arrived to get everything sorted out. He arrived at the gate and spoke into the speaker but nobody replied. For three hours he was there trying to get in but no-one would answer him. After panicking and phoning the Training Major up, telling him that he couldn't get in to the training area, he remembered the phone call when he first booked it. He then spoke in to the speaker and said,

'The milk bottles are empty.'

With that, the officer in charge of the training area said,

'Pleased to see you, I'll be down in five minutes to let you in.' He wouldn't have let him in unless he had said the code words and had been watching him for three hours on the cameras. On another occasion another Sergeant Major and I directed every phone in the head-quarters to the adjutant's phone. I was pissing myself every time his phone rang, about every ten seconds, especially when I heard him say,

'What the fuck is going on? Why is the cleaner's son phoning me to find out what time she will be home?'

This went on all day until the RSM told him what we had done, he took it well and just called us a pair of twats. We also started the phantom raspberry blower and used to phone everyone up and just raspberry them. This went on for about two weeks and even the CO mentioned it on his weekly meeting, saying,

'If I find who is responsible, I'll charge them.'

The suspicion started to fall on me so I got my mate to phone the adjutant when I was in his office. It was really hard not to laugh when he answered his phone and got raspberried, I heard him say,

'I don't believe it! I have been raspberried again!'

It took the suspicion off me, I know it was childish but kept me and my mate entertained for weeks. The RSM got hold of us and said,

'I know it's you two twats, I suggest you stop!'

So to be on the safe side we quit our little joke.

I had some spare time, so I got myself on a two week football coaching course. I thought it would be easy and I would learn how to carry the bucket and give a good team talk. How wrong I was, it just happened I did it when the Army team was doing the course as well. I was the oldest and the least skilful and got beasted for the whole two weeks. I could not stand on my legs after each day of being on the football field, running around all day with fit twenty year olds. To make it to the Army team you have to be skilful and I was nowhere near their standard.

I was posted to the TA to teach them a new computer system. I had been taught it on a one year course and only had six weeks' training on it; I never thought I'd need to use it again. In the Army as you pass Sergeant rank you normally do a job for about two years, get good at it and then get sent to do a different one after a short course, and start again. You have to be very adaptable, I didn't have a clue about it but I had to learn fast and bluff my way through it. I spent nights sitting in the back of an armoured vehicle, revising it all. I had to write the database for the computer system and if I got it wrong the rounds would have landed everywhere. The first time the Regiment fired using it I was crapping myself but it actually worked. After all the training they decided that they were getting rid of the system and took it all back. What a waste of tax payers' money, and two years of my hard work.

My two next door neighbours had unlucky experi-ence. One had lost his leg whilst in Bosnia; he was in a building when it was hit by an anti-tank round and his leg was blown off in the explosion. The other neigh-bour had just been shot twice in Northern Ireland. He decided to go parachuting to get his confidence back but all he did, on his first jump, was end up breaking his back. I must admit when I saw him I could not help but laugh my head off. Whilst here I also had to take a lot of Chelsea Pensioners to a function, on the way home they all ended up fighting each other and caused a riot in the mini bus. The one who was sitting next to me pissed himself and I got wet through. I looked at him and said,

'You dirty bastard!'

'When you are my age, son,' he replied, 'you'll do the same.'

As I dropped them back at the barracks they were still at it. The man in charge said they were always like that when they were pissed, apparently all of them are a bloody nightmare when they had been drinking.

The RSM got hold of three tickets to do the London marathon, I thought it would be a good idea to have a go at it as I'd never run that far before. We came up with a great training programme that we never stuck to. I had so many other commitments and my interpretation of the training consisted of three ten mile runs, lots of quarter pounders with cheese, strawberry milkshakes and lots of cigars. At the start everyone was looking rather professional and warming up, I stood there with a cigar in my mouth, my warm up consisting of me doing my shoe laces up and pinning my number to my t-shirt. I ran the marathon and started slow as I had not done it before, I couldn't believe it when people were dropping out in the early stages; they looked like professional runners to me. At the seventeen mile mark my adjutant said he had to stop and walk and for me to carry on without him. I looked at him and said,

'If you walk now, every morning I will come to your office, shake my head and look at you with no respect, and make sure every officer in the Corps knows you are a fanny!'

He replied, 'You're a bastard, Sergeant Major!' and I replied,

'Yes I am sir, now keep running and don't be a poof.'

To his credit he carried on and completed it without walking. I finished it in four hours, I only found it painful at the seventeen mile mark; if I had trained I think I would have done it a lot faster. We raised £1500 for a children's charity, so the pain was worth it. Not long after, I was posted back to my regiment after two happy years and good fun.

The regiment was posted to Bosnia on a peace keeping tour, basically this was to keep the peace between the different ethnic groups. I had to go on a week's pre-operational tour course, where you were refreshed on your shooting skills and did things like mine clearance as this was a major threat out there. The tour was classed as an operational tour but to be honest we got a medal for doing very little, we just had to help to rebuild the country. It was all due to the break-up of Yugoslavia and the different regions wanting independence, the country is a lovely place but unfortunately towns were still damaged from the war. If a building had a picture of a woman on it, it meant that women had been raped in it or killed. It was the same if it had a picture of a baby on it; it was quite revolting to see and reminded you of the cruel world we sometimes live in. People always complain about our soldiers having to go to far off places to fight and maybe die, but when you know that thousands of innocent people, including children, have been murdered, every British soldier would volunteer to go and risk his life to try and stop it. Europe sat around for too long letting this happen and it was only due to the Americans and British having the balls to send their troops in that it did stop. A lot of soldiers died out there, it was mainly due to the road conditions and having fatal accidents. Nearly every road had a monument to a British soldier who had been killed on it. There were lots of mountains and small tracks that got very dangerous in bad weather; it was extremely cold as well. I mentioned about we were given medals for this tour, in my opinion, it wasn't worth one as the fighting had stopped when we were there just trying to rebuild the country.

After the Gulf War people who were serving on a United Nations peace keeping tour in Cyprus were awarded the Gulf War medal, they were hundreds of miles away but as they were in range of scud missiles, they were awarded the same medal as those who had done the fighting. The only difference was that they did not have a rosette on their ribbon. All I did on that tour was help run an artillery range for six months, and I was awarded a medal for it. I have five medals but I can say the only ones I really earned were the Gulf War and the Long Service ones; I believe that some medals are deserved and should be worn with pride, but others aren't.

After this tour I was selected for the position of Battery Sergeant Major. I was the top soldier in the battery and in charge of about one hundred and twenty men. I ran the battery with my Battery Commander. Before I took up the post I had to attend a course where you were told about facts and figures and had to sit in lectures. You weren't tested or taught anything, but spent the nights drinking until the early hours. At the end of it the man in charge of the course interviewed me and said I would do well as a Battery Sergeant Major and good luck. This was my first taste of someone being two faced and someone who tried to ruin my career for no reason. I arrived back at my regiment and my Regimental Sergeant Major called me into his office. He told me to read a letter to him from this individual. It was two pages of him abusing me, saying I was crap and a total waste of space and should not be a Battery Sergeant Major (he obviously did not like me). When the Battery Sergeant Major Board sat, forty four BSMs were selected from about two hundred names. I came fourteenth: this was scored from my reports and past performance, five independent Colonels were involved so why he said what he said about me after only seeing me sitting in lectures, I couldn't understand. The RSM was a good, kind lad and said,

'Just prove him wrong. I will not put this letter in your file as it could be read by the Commanding Officer, he then could take it into consideration if he wanted to look at you for future promotions.'

He said he'd keep it in his draw and if I proved him wrong he would put it in the bin. He kept his word and four months later called me in to his office and said I was doing really well, and put the letter in the bin.

The Commanding Officer took an immediate dislike to me and it was lucky that he was posted as my career was saved. The role of this job is excellent, when you suddenly realise how much power you have you have to be careful to remember your fundamental aim. You need to get to know all your men inside and out to make sure your Battery performs well. Then to be considered for promotion to RSM, you have to make it to number one in the Regiment. This was a task in itself, but it didn't actually concern me too much as I knew that if you did your job well, more would come your way (my priority was to make sure my men performed and I did my best to look after them and advance their careers). A lot of men who were given this honour to command often forgot their priority; their only concern was to think about their future and not the promotion of others. To have any chance of making it to Regimental Sergeant Major, you have to be number one or two in your regiment. It's at this stage that your Commanding Officer starts to groom you and gets you noticed by all the top ranking officers, people who could have an input on the boards and who could be marking your reports. You also get put under pressure and hit with all sorts of high profile activities to see if you can perform them well. A lot of men crack under the pressure. I used to watch them sit behind a computer all day until late at night. I told my Battery Clerk that if I spent more than hour at the computer he would be sacked because his job was to type and do the paper work and my job was to look after my soldiers. He did try to commit suicide, I sound harsh in some of my statements but that's the way it is. To make it to the top you have to be a shrewd cookie and focus on the tasks and things that were going to help not hinder. Maybe if I'd spent more time typing, he would have been happier, but English isn't my strong point and that was not directly helping my soldiers. It's all about having the balls to delegate and trusting your men to perform well and complete the task without dropping you in it. You must be prepared for your soldiers to make mistakes but they also must know that they don't make the same mistake twice. If the Battery makes a mistake it all comes down to the Battery Sergeant Major and the Battery Commander, so your leadership strategies are extremely important, fair but firm and you have to make sure your Battery is the best at soldiering and on the sports field.

You have so much power every soldier beneath you stands to attention and calls you sir, if you ask someone to report to your office, they stand there with fear if it is for a bollocking, or respect if it's to give them an order to carry out some work. Basically what you say goes; if you want to make something happen then it happens. My favourite saying was 'adapt and overcome, just get it done'. It is so important to make your soldiers stand out in the regiment and do your best for them so they get noticed and get promoted. You must put them first and pass on your knowledge to them and give them responsibility. Unfortunately this does not always happen and some Sergeant Majors try and take all the glory and use it just as a stepping stone for their own career.

When I took over the battery I had to make lots of changes to get it the way I wanted, for the first three months it was hell and I thought everyone hated me, I spent just about every day bollocking someone and getting on everyone's case to get them educated in how I wanted the battery to run. We had a function and all the soldiers came up to me and said that I had got the battery back on its feet and I was doing a great job, this was a great feeling as I'd been a total dictator but it had all paid off as there was respect on both sides.

One of my roles was to sort out orders when a soldier was having disciplinary action taken against him. I always tried my best not to have to put a soldier on orders as it involved so much paperwork, but there are times when a soldier has to be punished for a crime. I remember one occasion when my Battery Commander came in in his tracksuit, and I said,

'Don't forget we got your orders in five minutes.'

'Don't worry, I'll be ready,' he reassured me. I knew he had forgotten about it, but I briefed the soldier and got him ready to be marched in to the Battery Commander's Office. I opened his door and said,

'Are you ready?'

'Yes, let's crack on,' he replied. We went through the procedure and as he talked to the soldier about his sentence I looked at the floor and noticed his boots were still there. I then looked at him behind his desk and he still had his trainers and shorts on. He had only had the time to put his army top on, I couldn't help but laugh and when it was time to march the soldier out I was giggling uncontrollably, the poor soldier must have thought I was laughing at his sentence.

You get a lot of young soldiers who are trouble makers and are just waiting for their three years to be up, so they can get out of the Army. On one occasion I received a phone call from the police saying that they had one of my soldiers who had been caught trying to get away without paying to fill his car up with fuel. The policeman said they would let him off as he was a soldier, and let us deal with him. I told the policeman the soldier was a total waste of rations and I would like them to deal with it, this was because we actually wanted him out. We got rid of him in the end as I always believed if you have a bad apple you should get rid of it before it spreads badness.

I had to bollock a soldier and I ended up calling him a 'fucking knob'. He reported me for racism, saying I had called him a nig nog. The thing I did not understand about it was that he was bloody white, fortunately nothing came of it and I managed to get him posted out of the regiment.

My battery was then sent to Kosovo on another operational tour, this was about the same as the Bosnia tour and I was given another medal for doing very little. My job here was to collect all the weapons handed in by the locals. They all had them, most of them dated from the Second World War. I used to send them down to the Greeks who would put them in a big furnace and burn them. Some of the weapons were worth thousands of pounds, like the old Tommy guns that you see on the gangster films. They were parachuted into the country by the Americans during the Second World War for the patricians to use against the Germans. Every individual had a weapon as it was in their culture to have them; it was important to try and disarm them so they stopped using them on each other.

I also looked after the Kosovo Army weapons as they weren't allowed to have them without our say so. It was a pain in the arse having to count over five thousand weapons on a weekly basis. In my opinion it wasn't a job for a Battery Sergeant Major but that's what I was told to do, so that's the way it was. I also had to do random checks on the weapons we had issued to their soldiers. On one occasion I turned up at their barracks and told them I was there to do a check, I was surrounded by twenty of their elite soldiers, all of whom had done a lot of fighting in the war and wouldn't think twice about putting a knife across my throat. It was one of those occasions you had to be firm and use all your experience and training to defuse the situation. I told them I was not going until I had checked them, and that my signaller would call for reinforcements if they didn't get their Commanding Officer now. They thought about it and I found myself in the Commanding Officer's Office, drinking coffee with him apologising for the situation. That was one of the scariest times in my career, twenty well trained men surrounding me with anger in their eyes. Their CO said to me,

'It's because you are a Sergeant Major that we dealt with you with respect. If you had been a young officer the outcome could have been very different, but we know what rank you are and what you have done to get to the rank so we respect you.'

On one occasion a Dutch officer asked to borrow two pistols that had been handed in so he could bury them and use them for training his search dogs. These dogs were trained to sniff out weapons and used to go into local houses to find weapons that were being hidden. I allowed him to borrow two pistols that he buried and left over night. When he turned up in the morning he found to his horror that the locals had tarmacked and were started to build a road exactly where the pistols were buried. There were a lot of explanations and reports to be made out to explain the whereabouts of the two missing pistols. They are still buried under a road in Kosovo somewhere.

After this tour when we were back in England on a Friday night I had a phone call. I was told that the Commanding Officer wanted me and the Battery Commander in his office straight away. When we arrived we were given instructions to get the battery ready to move to help with the floods in York. You can imagine getting hold of one hundred men on a Friday night just as they had been paid. The system did actually work and somehow we managed to get everyone from the battery ready to deploy at 0900hrs the next day. Of course some of them had a lot of sobering up to do. And they were not happy when the Sergeants turned up in the local bars and chucked them in the back of a Land Rover to take them back to camp. We were deployed to help with the floods in York for three days, the lads liked this as it was different to their everyday work and most of the public appreciated us. We basically spent three days filling sandbags and then placing them as barricades wherever they were needed. I had to calm a situation down when a twat mouthed it off to one of my soldiers about how he was finally getting his money worth from his taxes, as he stood there watching the soldiers build a wall of sandbags around his house. As expected the lads wanted to drop him so I had to tell the man to get back in his house for his own safety. I added he'd be getting his money's worth from the NHS as well if he didn't wise up, this he did and nothing was heard from him again. Sometimes I used to cringe at the stupidity of men, he would have caused so much hassle if he hadn't obeyed instructions to go in.

It was around about this time more women were joining up; I feel women do have a role in the army, particularly as medics, drivers and signallers. There are obvious problems such as maternity leave and in my opinion some were not able to do as much of the physical work. If the shit hit the fan and you were in a trench would you want a woman next to you; if you were being attacked by ten six foot men would you want a woman to fight your corner? But I feel they have their place. It was proven that pilots were more relaxed when it was a women's voice talking to them on the radio. Also gay people were now allowed to join; but if they could do the work I wouldn't find it a problem. Reading this you might think I was homophobic, or wouldn't have women on my team, that's just not true. I will say that whoever they were, if they were not up to scratch I would kick them into touch. You have to have confidence that the people with you can look after themselves and would watch your back if the shit hit the fan.

In the Army you have different appointments per rank, so you can be the same rank but senior by appointment. For example, a Warrant Officer Class Two could be a Troop Warrant Officer, who is less senior to a Battery Warrant Officer, who is less senior to a Regimental Quarter Master – but you all hold the same rank. After my two year tour as the Battery Sergeant Major I was given the Regimental Quarter Master Sergeant technical job. The Regimental Quarter Master Sergeant Majors are the Senior Warrant Officer Class Two appointments in the regiment. This job was a nightmare. I had to do a six week course (they might as well been talking in Latin as I did not understand any of it), but somehow bluffed my way through it again. It was here that I looked out of the classroom window and was watching a man driving a lawn mower, he was cutting the grass on the sports field at the time. I wished I was doing that job instead of being in there listening to someone speaking to me in a different language. Little did I know this was the first seed to be planted in my head for my career in Civvie Street in my next life. On taking up this appointment I found that I had to rely on my store man underneath me. They were the experts as they had done this job for years, so sometimes I would have to ask for their advice:

they were technically better than I was, even though they were a lower rank. How could I have known as much as they did from just doing a six week course?

It was at this stage my officer told me he was going away on a promotion course for six months, and I would be doing his job as well. It was the first job that I used to go home with a head ache from the amount of paper work and just general pressure. I wasn't experienced in that type of work and I could feel it. The highlight of that post was doing the fire strike. We were on exercise in Canada again and were told that we were on standby for the strike. Some of the key heads of departments were flown home straight away to prepare, and I was one of them. On my first day back in England I arrived at camp to find sixty Green Goddess fire engines sitting there ready for me to take over and then issue to the fire crews. The Quartermaster, four other Sergeant Majors and I had to go and do a recce of where all the lads were going to be based. The Quartermaster, in charge of all the vehicles in the regiment, told the driver to go through the tunnel in the regiment's mini bus. The driver looked at him and said,

'Sir, the tunnel is not wide or high enough for us to fit through!'

'Don't be stupid,' the Quartermaster replied, 'just drive through!' We got to the other end and the roof had been taken off and the sides crushed in. We were now in an open top bus. The driver looked at the Quartermaster and before he could say anything the Quartermaster said

'No-one say a fucking thing.' Obviously we were all pissing ourselves, the Quartermaster had to donate some money to charity and it was all kept quiet. The next day he put petrol in a diesel engine so he did not have a good two days.

The lads loved doing this job and could not see what the firemen were complaining about. On one occasion one of the lads was bored so he phoned up emergency services (999), saying there was a fire at his old school, an absolutely stupid thing to do. His fire engine was called to the school and it was found to be a hoax. The call was tracked down to him and he was given a month in jail (he had only done it as he wanted his teachers to see how well he was doing for himself, his brains were obviously in his little toe as he was not doing so well after that incident). I used to have to go on the Commanding Officer's weekly meeting to all the head of departments in the Regiment, as my officer was away. I remember one meeting I was just day dreaming as the Commanding Officer was going on about some issue when I suddenly heard him say,

'What do you think, RQ? And how do you think we should go about it?'

'Shit!' I thought, what was he talking about, how can I bluff my way out of this one? Well I couldn't, and had to say,

'Sorry sir, you got me when my mind was elsewhere and I haven't a clue what you are talking about.' I was expecting to get a massive bollocking but he burst into laughter, and so did everyone else around the table. He said,

'You won't do that again, will you RQ?' and carried on with the meeting.

I seemed to get hammered to do everything during this period, but realise now it was the Regiment trying to show my profile off so I could stand the chance of promotion. If any officer came to visit the Regiment I had to meet and greet them so they knew who I was. I also had to stand in for the RSM when he was away so I was slowly getting groomed.

At the end of the strike I was promoted to Warrant Officer Class One Regimental Sergeant Major. I remember having promotion drinks in the Mess and sitting on the toilet, extremely pissed, at 11 o'clock in the morning, just looking at my Regimental Sergeant Major badge. I couldn't believe it I had made it to top soldier; all my dreams had come true. I was posted to the Battle Group Training Unit on Salisbury Plain, typical it was the one job that I did not want, we all seemed to be posted to places we did not want to go to.

This was where the Battle Groups came along and were tested on exercises, by this time in my army career I was quite used to doing as I was told even if it was the worst job and I didn't want to do it.

Before I was posted to my new unit a couple of the lads took me out for a quiet drink down the local town, the night was quiet, that was until we ended up in a chip shop to get some food (we decided we'd fill our stomachs before crashing out). A couple of girls were in there being loud so my mate said something which offended them, he called one of them 'mate' (she had short hair); he made out he thought she was a man (in his eyes an easy mistake to make and very entertaining from our point of view). He said sorry straight away, but was clearly not in their good books. A big lad came in and started talking to the girls, and then shouted out,

'Don't worry, I'll sort them out!'

Obviously the girls had said something to him. We did then just ignore them, I could see my mate was getting angry and came out with,

'You know what pisses me off? When men mouth it off to look hard in front of women!'

'You're hard because there are three of you,' the big lad said.

'No just me, they went outside,' my mate replied. The big lad tried hitting my mate but my mate just stood there and somehow managed to get his hands close enough to play with his nipples. The big lad couldn't understand what was going on, he was trying to hit my mate whilst he just played with his nipples. My mate eventually got bored and hit him, with one punch he was finished and that was the end of that. I think the big lad learnt a lesson not to mouth it off again.

Before I took over my post as a Regimental Sergeant Major I had to go to London for a week where all the out-going and in-coming RSMs meet. Of course there is loads of drinking and lectures but you also get a lot of VIP treatment. We were taken to the Tower of London; I sat in the House of Commons, I was amazed and in awe of what was happening. At the dinner night a letter is read out from the Queen wishing all her RSMs a great night. It's now that you have reached the big time and the importance and responsibility that go with the rank and appointment hits home.

I started my new posting. The first stage was a four day hand over by the outgoing RSM. And then it was down to doing the job that I had always aimed for.

When I arrived at my new posting there was a retired colonel there, in my opinion he had a chip on his shoulder; he was a civilian who talked to everybody as though he was still the top man. I could not under-stand why all the serving Majors were letting this retired Colonel talk to them like a piece of rubbish (I'd been briefed by the previous RSM that he was trouble and they had had a lot of run ins). I was expecting him to start on me one day, and this happened after six weeks in my new job. One day I was walking along the corridor when he said,

'Can I have a word, RSM?'

Out of politeness I called him sir, even though he was a retired Colonel and a civilian working for the Army. He started arguing with me and screaming like a girl. I had a go back, and told him he was acting like a girl or going through his monthly cycle. I reminded him he was a civilian, which he hated this as nobody had done that to him before. I could not believe he was talking to the top soldier as though he was a pissant. I went and saw my Colonel and said,

'You need to back me and sort him out.'

To his credit he did and the ex-Colonel left shortly afterwards. As soon as you have the badge of rank on your arm you are treated like a god, it was great. The power you have is amazing. If you want something to happen, it happens, if you voice an opinion, you are listened to. You and the Commanding Officer are the face of the Regiment; it is important that the two of you have total respect and trust for each other. The RSM has to be one hundred percent loyal to his CO and inform him of everything you know, so he's in the know. A good CO will listen to what the RSM has to say and then make his opinion from there. There were a number of occasions where the relationship was not formed and Regimental Sergeant Majors were removed from their post and their careers ended. It is not easy to remove an RSM from his post but this has happened. Unfortunately due to personal problems that happened in my life, that I will mention in the next chapter, I had to make the hard decision to end my career and had to decide if it was time to leave the Army.

As an RSM I played a management role, it was really a bigger version of when I was a BSM. Normally after reaching the rank of WO1 RSM you get commissioned and could do another fifteen years in the Army. For most soldiers your career ends after twenty two years' service and you have no option but to retire (the Army is in no shadow of a doubt a young man's game). The reason you only do two years as a RSM is that the Army has to keep the promotion ladder rolling. When a WO1 retires it means that a WO2 is promoted to WO1, a Staff Sergeant is promoted to WO2, a Sergeant is promoted to Staff Sergeant, a Bombardier is promoted to Sergeant, a Lance Bombardier is promoted to Bombadier and a Gunner is promoted to Lance Bombardier. If you did not have this system in place you would have people waiting a long time to be promoted. People would be less motivated and those in the lower ranks would be a lot older. Like I mentioned before, it is the lower ranks in the early years of their careers that do the fighting, the foot patrols and the real soldiering. So they need to be young and fit, not a bunch of forty years olds. The young soldier must also have a good chance of getting promoted: this keeps him focused on doing his best at all times. Take the promotion away and he will just plod along waiting to draw his pension at the age of retirement.

CHAPTER NINE

Grief

This chapter shows how you never know what is around the corner when you think your life is ticking along nicely, and how it can be suddenly changed and you feel like you've been kicked in the bollocks. I learnt this lesson; it was a hard one. In my opinion the worst thing that can happen to a dad, happened to me. I had to end my career due to a build-up of personal problems that happened over the last five years of my career. They started as I took over the Battery Sergeant Major appointment. I had just taken over the role of Battery Sergeant Major, I'd made it to the top soldier in the Battery, and everything I had worked so hard for had led to this point. This appointment is where you have to be at the top of your game, with the Battery Commander you are the face of the Battery and everything that happens is down to your management skills. You are also under the microscope by the CO and RSM and everything you do is noticed, whether it's good or bad. You are the top soldier of a unit; it was a unit rich in history in my case, going back to the war in the Americas and one of the Battery's soldiers winning the Victoria Cross in the Crimea. The soldier concerned won the Victoria Cross when he managed to keep his gun firing even though he had been bayoneted thirteen times. Whilst I was the BSM his grave was found in an overgrown cemetery in Portsmouth, I sent some members of the battery to sort it out and now every Remembrance Day two members of the battery go to Portsmouth and lay a wreath on his grave. You are looked at as though you know everything and it is not a time to have personal problems in your life: the job is hard enough even when everything is going well.

One lunch time I was running around the air field. I did this every lunch time as I had to keep up with my soldiers, and had to work a bit harder to maintain my fitness. This was definitely harder the older I was. Being the top soldier you have to lead from the front, of course you are not going to be the fastest but you must be in the top twenty percent or you will lose respect of the men underneath you. On this occasion I bumped in to an old friend who was also running, I said to him,

'Life is great, I've just taken over the role of Battery Sergeant Major and after this run I am going to hospital to see my daughter being born!'

I already had two sons and was really excited about having a daughter. My daughter was born, but within twenty four hours it was obvious that something was not quite right with her. She was rushed to the intensive care unit in Middlesbrough and I remember following the ambulance with its flashing lights and siren going, with tears in my eyes. Within about eighteen hours being born she started to have a major fit. I watched helplessly as she fitted for hours with the doctors trying to figure out what was wrong with her. If an adult is ill I would say well they had a good life, but to watch a young child, especially when it's your own flesh and blood, is the most heart breaking experience I have ever had been through. She spent about three days in intensive care; this was a horrid experience as you are surrounded by other parents who are going through the same as you.

When I looked at my new baby in an incubator with all sorts of tubes going into her I felt terrible. The doctors were telling me she would be alright, they thought it was just a reaction to some medicine and they could not find anything wrong with her. She was moved out of intensive care into a normal ward and I started to feel relief, but little did I know this was the start of something else that would leave me completely out of my depth. After two weeks of constant tests and scans the doctor asked me to follow him into a room, where he sat me down. I knew it was going to be bad as he had two nurses in with him. He drew a picture of a brain and then drew big black circles in it, saying,

'I am sorry to say, but your daughter's brain looks like this, the black circles are all damaged parts. She might be physically or mentally damaged but at this stage we don't know.'

The amount of damage to her brain looked terrible: it looked like about forty percent had been damaged. I asked what had caused it and they said they were sorry but there was no explanation, it was just one of those things that happen. They thought that somewhere along the line she was starved of oxygen. I walked out and once on my own in my car I broke down and cried like a baby. When I arrived home I sat in the garage for about three days, just smoking cigars and trying to get in my head what had happened This is the way I deal with things as bad as this, I can't be doing with other people, I just need to be on my own. Unless you have had a child where you are told they are likely to die, you would have no idea of that pain. It is taken for granted your child will be born well but it is more common than you think for this sort of tragedy to take place. I decided you could crumble or be strong, it was shit but it had been dealt and I had to deal with it. I then decided on the policy to treat her as a normal child.

Two weeks later I went back to the hospital where the doctor told me it was worse than they thought, and that there was twice as much damage as they had first thought. They said that they didn't think she would be able to do anything mentally or physically, and she would die young as there was so much damage in her brain. I had been kicked in the teeth many times in my life but this was definitely top in the list of pain. To hold your baby in your arms knowing she is very ill makes you feel so helpless, they say there is a god up there but if so, why would he let a little girl be born like this and then have to live a life of illness and pain? All I can say if there is anyone up there he's not a good man.

I cracked on and started the life of hospital appointments and sleepless nights looking after my baby girl. She was named Lucy. I ended up with about two hours' sleep at night as she needed twenty four hour care. I did this and I did it well if I may say so myself, I still managed to do my job well and look after the children with no major problems. I would be up with her until five in the morning, get two hours' sleep and be at work for seven o'clock, sometimes then I'd go on a five mile run with my Battery. I told my RSM that I wanted to be treated the same as anyone else, I told him I would do my job well and I wanted no special treatment. He expressed his concern for me and my daughter and was very supportive.

'Fine,' he said, 'but let me know if it gets too much for you.'

My RSM was good and gave me time off to take her to hospital appointments etc., and I caught up with the work I missed at night. Often soldiers would come to me and tell me their problems, and I used to reply,

'Have you a daughter who is going to die? Well, I have and I'm not moaning, just cracking on! Is your problem as bad as that?'

With that they would usually realise their problem was not a problem and they'd just get on with it, I think the fact that I did one of the senior jobs well under a difficult personal position was courageous, if I may say so myself. The trauma of my daughter's illness showed them how insignificant their issues were in the bigger scale of things. One thing that was for sure, it made them stop and think.

It was hard when it came to stages in Lucy's development, where normal children would walk and learn to talk, I knew she should but wouldn't, when she should be sitting up she wasn't, I just got on with it and gave her all the love I could. I asked the doctors if we were safe to have another child and were told yes as this was just a one-off incident, so three years later we did.

My son was born just as I started my job as the RSM. He was called James. I looked at him and thought thank god he was ok. I went home and in the morning got a phone call saying I needed to get to the hospital straight away. I arrived at the hospital and was told it had happened again, I couldn't believe it. I went through the whole procedure again, watching him fit and being put into intensive care. On one occasion we watched him being resuscitated. They did investigations and they found out that my children had a rare genetic disease called pyruvate dehydrogenase deficiency, this is where they haven't the battery inside them to produce energy; it was so rare that there were only twenty more in the world. The children are totally disabled and need twenty four hour care. They are fed through their stomachs via a tube. Lucy is blind and James can only see out of one eye, and they can't talk. It was unlucky we both had the bad gene and it was passed on to our children, lots of other couples have the same bad gene but it only comes out one in four children, if we had only had our two first children we would have never known. My children have a life limiting condition, I can't explain what the feeling is like to be in this position, it hurts. My way of dealing with it is to treat them like normal children and do my best so when they die I can hold my head up and say I did everything I could for them.

I was working in the south of England and I only came home at weekends. My ex wife was left at home in Newark with the two ill children as I only came home at weekends. On one of these occasions I came home as usual. She looked like death from only getting a few hours' sleep at night, and from the pressure of all the care she had to do. I decided to leave the Army. Being away eight months of the year was not me doing my best for my children. I wanted to spend as much time with them as possible. I knew that I had very little time with them: being a soldier and being away from them for eight months a year was not something I could do any more. If I put myself first I would have felt like I hadn't been a good father, and I knew this would screw my head up on their deaths. So I did what I thought was the right thing and told the Army that I was going to leave when my twenty two years was up. I wasn't going to put myself into the frame for commission to Captain, this was what you normally did after being an RSM. It was so hard to go up to my Commanding Officer and tell him I had to call it a day, and that I needed a compassionate posting nearer to my home. The Army was so good and sorted a posting out for me so I could do a bit of work, but also be there for my children.

I have since realised that every family you speak to has had some sort of grief in their family history. I was speaking to one of my customers when he told me that his uncle survived being held prisoner by the Japanese, and on his return started a job working on the railways. The points were closed and he was caught in them. The work men could not free him in time before he was crushed by an oncoming train. I mentioned to my mate that I had just walked around the cemetery whilst I was waiting for my truck to have its MOT, and that I had noticed how many graves for young children were in there. He then told me his Aunt was in there as she had been murdered at the age of fourteen. The perpetrator was one of the last men to be hanged in Britain for this crime. A friend of mine went to the dentist for a check-up and was told his mouth was riddled with cancer. He was dead two years later, at the age of thirty. A relative of one of my children's carers reversed his car, killing his small child. These are just a few stories and show that most families have sad stories to tell, and what happened to me and my children is just another sad story that takes place in the circle of life.

I retrained as a Tree Surgeon and started my own business so I could still work and look after my children. When I bought my house I became a keen gardener, I didn't realise but this was to be the beginning of a new era. When I was gardening on my own house I thought to myself that I'd love to do it as a living. Later I was looking through some magazines and saw a picture of a man hanging from a tree, that's when I thought, 'That's it, that's what I want to do!' I got myself booked on the relevant courses and got the qualifications I needed and started my own business. It has been great fun and to be honest I enjoy it more than anything I did in the Army. I think this is because the intensity of being a soldier and the severe pressure that I was under got to me, but now it's a completely different story.

In the last three months of your Army career you are given time to get work, I used this time to set up my own business. I managed to get some spare time, a rarity in those days. I helped some friends who did night security at public events: protecting show grounds, etc.

The guy who I ended up working with had a flair for boxing and was dependable as a handy lad. About two in the morning on one occasion we found two young 'uns, who had sneaked into the show ground we were working at and were getting high on drugs. We had to escort them out of the show ground; one of them turned a knife out of his pocket and started shouting,

'I'm going to use it!'

'Just go away,' my mate said, but as the lad came towards us, he continued, 'before you showed the knife I was going to show you mercy. Now, no mercy!' And with that he hit him and knocked him out.

'It's normal at this stage I would stick the knife in your arse, to teach you a lesson,' my mate told him, 'but this time, I'll just get the police.'

We called the police and they arrested him. We found out he was on bail for stabbing someone three weeks earlier.

On one of the organised events a gypsy family turned up from Ireland, we refused them entry and the so-called 'king' started on my mate, yes you guessed it, they ended up having a good fight! Unfortunately I missed it all as I was in the shower, and of course I got severe abuse for not being there when needed. The family of travellers were used to people being scared of their reputation; they thought by intimidating us and by being violent they would get their own way. What they didn't realise was this time they had started on the wrong man; my mate did end up with a black eye, cut knuckles and a bad chest where a wheel brace had been used against him. But the gypsies did actually leave, and as they left there were shouts of 'I am still the king of the gypsies!' We spent the whole week at the gate armed with pick axes just in case they came back with more men.

When I went for my final medical with the Army, I had a broken ankle. I'd not listened to my climbing instructor. He'd told us not to be lazy and never use a ladder to climb a tree as they're dangerous, he told us to always use the climbing rope when climbing trees, and he was right. I used the ladder and it slipped. I broke my ankle and had to drive sixty miles to the A and E department; the pain of pushing the clutch in was horrendous. As I walked in to the doctor's treatment room for my medical with my leg in plaster and on crutches, he said,

'Get undressed.'

'Fuck off!' I replied, 'it took me forty five minutes to get dressed with this plaster, just put me down as fit!' I thought it was just another chance to grab my balls and look up my backside. 'I am as fit and slim as the day I joined,' I protested, but at this point he told me that I weighed in at fourteen and half stone, five stone heavier than my first medical at sixteen (no wonder the fitness test hurt me in my later years, it was the equivalent of running around the mile and half with a five stone man in my arms).

The one thing I do not miss is having to keep extremely fit. As you get older, you get fatter and slower. They do give you longer to complete your run, and you don't have to do as many press ups and sit ups on the fitness tests. On other occasions you did PT with the young soldiers and you still had to keep up with them and lead by example (I am fit, but must admit it took me a lot of effort to keep the standard up). Doing three PT lessons a week with the Army was not enough and I found that I had to put in another three sessions on my own. I was looking forward to eating cream cakes and not having to worry about it. I remember my RSM telling me to lose two stone or buy another Mess Dress. I took the easy option, but it cost me another four hundred pounds to buy a new uniform.

I hope this shows anybody who is reading this that you never know what is around the corner, so when you worry about all the stupid things that really don't matter just remember there are ill people out there and as long as you have got your health then that's all that matters. Without that you have nothing. When my friend's father died, his last words were,

'Remember: nothing matters; nothing is important.'

I think those words are so true.

CHAPTER TEN

Civvie Street

After twenty three years and eleven months of Army service, now at the age of forty, weighing fourteen and a half stone (all pure muscle of course), I left the Army and moved to a new area. I didn't know anyone and I had no contacts. I knew by hard work, personality and determination I would make my business work. I bought a truck, tools and put an advert in the paper, all that was left was to wait for the phone to ring. Thankfully it did, and my business was begun. I wanted to make money but still be able to care for my ill children; this job enabled me to be flexible for hospital appointments, etc. I knew it would be hard (or even impossible) to be in a job where I had to go up to a boss to ask for time off when my children were ill. Being my own boss took that problem away and to be honest after twenty three years in the Army, the thought of being on my own, climbing trees in the wilderness, appealed to me. It gets lonely at times and when the work is slack I often think it would be good to be in a team again, having a laugh, but then I remember the stress that also went with it and remember how lucky I am to be doing what I am doing. I know there are thousands of people stuck behind a desk all day who would give anything to do what I am doing now. I can do this as I'm still fit, strong and healthy. I have always said a man needs three things, to love, to be loved and to have a reason to get up in the morning, i.e., work!

I still have a good laugh, when I was cleaning my teeth one morning I heard my girlfriend scream from the bedroom,

'I can't believe it, the dog has weed all over my feet!'

I found this hilarious, but must admit the day after, I woke up to a turd lying on my pillow and I wasn't so impressed. My humour was stretched and I told her we would be selling her on eBay.

People always say Civvie (Civilian) Street is hard after being in the Army. I think you couldn't be more wrong, I have found life a lot easier, the only thing I have noticed is there are a lot more people with bad attitudes around. In the Army the bad ones are controlled by the discipline, but in Civvie Street the bad ones are allowed to do what they want. The only deterrent I can see is that people can be arrested, and even then nothing seems to happen to them. I have been shocked by the amount of angry people I have come across since leaving the Army. Maybe this is due to the lack of discipline in their lives, or maybe they have just not come across people who have stood up to them, and they are used to acting like idiots. I was shocked when I used to watch my son play football and had to listen to how foul-mouthed some of the parents were.

I have also come across some great characters and nice people as well. Army life is hard. You could be away eight months a year, the work you do is hard and you are putting your life on the line for others who can't defend themselves. Your life is never settled as you never know what you are going to be doing as it can change daily. You do things that you don't want to do. You work hours that most people could not handle. The discipline is like nothing in any other organisation. You cannot say, 'No, I am not doing it,' and just look for another job: if you break the rules you are punished and could end up in a military prison. You are in environment where if you get it wrong, people die. You are expected to adapt and produce results under any condition. If you don't your career stops. When things go wrong, you have to come up with a plan and carry on. You can't say 'I can't do it,' because if you do they will just get someone who can. It is a good life for fit men with a sense of duty. You will never experience the same comradeship and fun anywhere else. There are days when you get lots of time off and life is easy, but it's the old saying, you train hard, work hard but also play hard. The Army gives everyone the same chance. It trains you, looks after you and welcomes you in to the family. The bond you have with your comrades stays with you for life.

Yes, you still have arseholes in the Army but the good people are good. I don't worry about much now. If I make a mistake no-one is going to die, but in the Army if I made just one that could have happened. That is pressure you work under. The experience of having two ill children changed my views on life and realised how lucky I was to be happy and healthy. In the Army you are doing a violent job surrounded by motivated men. This life makes you hard: you are trained to be aggressive and trained to kill, but the experience of my children has softened me. Whenever I see ill kids I find it hard to stop tears coming from my eyes.

Only today did I see a ill child in somebody's arms and tears ran down my cheek. I believe villains should go and spend a few days in the presence of these children. I am sure it would change their lives. Those who don't change should be sent to a quarry with a ball and chain, fed bread and water until they do.

My life as a tree surgeon has been great. I did break my ankle that once and had to drive sixty miles home with it, which was not fun, but apart from that it has been good. It is also as dangerous as anything I did in the Army, so the excitement is still there. If you fall from a tree you are going to die so you have to be switched on at all times. If you make a mistake with a chainsaw you will take a limb off. Civilian Street was what I needed after twenty three years' service and I am glad I did not go down the route of being commissioned and doing another fifteen years.

You hear stories of men that leave the Army, can't cope and end up living on the streets. You probably find that a lot of them couldn't cope with the Army and that's why they left. Either that or they were kicked out. Yes, there will be those who were good soldiers but found it hard to adapt, but most people I know have done extremely well on leaving and made it to high positions within their chosen career.

After twenty four years you get a good pension as well, which makes life good. Where else at the age of forty would you be given a lump sum and a pension payment every month until you die? I would say that you have earned it and have probably put your life on the line a few times, and spent eight months a year away from home. The Army is a young man's game and that's why you get a good pension at the age of forty. You wouldn't want overweight fifty year olds running into battle. This country is lucky that due to our history and culture you will always have men who will be willing to join up and fight for the people of this island. Those who think that it's a waste of tax payer's money should remember they have their freedom because of the young men that have done the business in the past, are doing it now and who will do it in the future. People must never take for granted the freedom they have in this country. To relax our guard would leave to some mad man in some part of the world taking that freedom away. Humans can be extremely cruel, foreign cultures are not always as seen on the holiday brochures this is why the country has war memorials in every town and city of this country.

One of the big things for success in Civvie Street is to get it in your head that you will no longer have people calling you sir, standing to attention and doing what you say. They are not interested in what you were. You have to remember that and realise you are just the same as everyone else. You do find those who can't do this and struggle. I live in a city and almost every week I see some angry twat get annoyed. Just the other day someone started on me for parking and getting in his way. I must admit I wanted to give him a good kicking, but let it go. I sometimes listen to people going on about what they have done and how great they are. I just get on with my life. If people want to think I am just some bod doing their garden or tree that's great, if they want to know more about me then I tell them what I did and what I achieved. As far as I am concerned now the soldier has gone and I am now the tree man.

Ten things a soldier must realise when he leaves the Army, to help him in Civilian Street:

1. If you get into a fight, the Sergeant Major will not ask if you won and congratulate you, instead the police will arrest you, and you will be punished.

2. Pain is not a weakness and will not go away on its own. It's not weak to go and get checked out by a doctor.

3. If you get so drunk that you piss your jeans you will not get a pat on your back. You will be looked at with disgust by the people around you. And probably arrested.

4. If you shout out, 'Naked bar!' and take your clothes off, you will be arrested.

5. If you get into debt, the Army will not bail you out. The bailiff will knock on your door.

6. If you come across someone being attacked or robbed and you step in to help, don't expect that those around you to help you. Expect them to watch when you get a kicking for your troubles.

7. If you hear a loud bang, such as a car back-fire, you are not to grab and then chuck those nearest to you to the ground, or look for cover and a good firing point. You will be arrested for assault.

8. Get used to people saying, 'Don't work too hard, take your time, you don't get paid any extra.'

9. You do not have to use starch on your jeans to put razor sharp creases in them. You will get arrested by the fashion police.

10. Always remember how fortunate you were to have served and met so many special comrades. When you feel low just remember some of the laughs you had and the special bond you will always have with those you served with.

Not a day goes by where I don't hear interesting stories. I got a burger from a van and whilst talking the man he told me he used to be a prison officer. I went back a week later for another burger and asked why he left the prison service. He told me that he was on duty when the IRA escaped. His team found them and one of his team was shot in the leg. They went in and he hit the IRA man over the head with the truncheon. All the IRA men were captured. The next day the ten prison wardens were told they had been accused of too much violence and were sent to a foreign country whilst it was sorted out. Meanwhile the IRA sent a black wreath to his family, stating that all his family members were going to die. In the end the charges against him were dropped but due to the government not backing him, all ten wardens left the service. My mate's brother spent five months on remand, having been accused of raping his wife. The case was dropped but he ended up being divorced and lost everything. He ended up living in a caravan that became his pride and joy. One day he awoke to a tapping at his window and was surprised to see a winch man from a helicopter. He looked down to see water pouring into his caravan. This was when the floods had hit Hull. He was winched to safety and as he looked down he said, 'Not my fucking caravan as well!' It was defiantly a Hamlet moment. These stories show that life still has a lot to throw at you. My years of army service were fantastic,

THE
BADGE

This hilarious and heart-breaking tale of life in the British Army charts soldier Ashley Topham's progress from scrawny troublemaker to Regimental Sergeant Major, wearer of The Badge, feared and respected by all.

From a comedy of errors resulting in his capture and interrogation by the KGB, to the triumph of his first operational combat, this absorbing story tells a soldier's life as it is, with all the unsavoury parts left in.

www.ashthebadge.com

9 781909 817074